Praise for Todd B. Natenberg

"This book shows you how to sell more and achieve all your income goals by reinventing yourself and your career!"

Brian Tracy
Author, *Maximum Achievement*

"Todd gives us a fresh approach that incorporates the proven fundamentals. He mixed the new with the old, the current with the proven. But unlike the thousands of other sales books on the market today, "I've been in sales for 10 years! Now what?" gives the proven professional tactics to take their business to the next level- that being of survival in today's market."

Roger Dawson
Author, *Secrets of Power Negotiating*

"If you're looking to reignite your sales career, buy this book. Breezy and fun to read, it's filled with ideas that—when acted on—will turbocharge your commissions and leave your customers smiling."

Pat Zigarmi
Co-Author, *Leadership and the One Minute Manager* and *Who Killed Change?*

"Todd has the greatest sales skills of anyone that I know. He is dedicated to helping others achieve their goals. AND, he understands sales!

Stephan Schiffman
Former President of DEI Management Group
Internationally known as "America's #1 Corporate Sales Trainer"

"Todd has exceptional sales skills. He understands the sales process, and knows how to execute a sales call. Todd also knows all of the little things like sending out agendas prior to a meeting and networking for referrals. Todd is a very passionate individual who brings a lot to an organization."

         Paul Rosen
         Senior Vice President of Sales, On Deck Capital

I've been in sales for 10 years! Now what?

A (NEW) PLAYBOOK FOR SKYROCKETING YOUR COMMISSIONS

Todd B. Natenberg

www.toddnatenberg.com
www.ijustgotajobinsales.com

Copyright © 2015 by Todd B. Natenberg
TBN Sales Solutions
5309 W. 153rd St.
Leawood, KS 66224
todd@toddnatenberg.com
www.ijustgotajobinsales.com
www.toddnatenberg.com
Natenberg, Todd
"I've been in sales for 10 years! Now what?" A (NEW) Playbook for Skyrocketing Your Commissions.
All rights reserved. No part of this book may be reproduced, translated, stored in a retrieval system, or transmitted in any form or by any means, electronic or otherwise, without prior permission in writing from the author.
ISBN#: 0974346942
TBN Sales Solutions
Leawood, KS
ISBN 13: 9780974346946

In memory of

T. Paul Natenberg
My beloved father

In death, you taught me how to live.

For my spectacular twin sons,

Ari and Teddy

What was it for Daddy when you were born?
Rebirth!

I love you more than anything in the whole wide world.
Home team!

And to my beautiful wife, Reena, who made it all possible.

I love you until the sun no longer sets, the stars no longer shine, the moon no longer glows, and the river no longer flows. I love you until forever.

Acknowledgments

If people had told me how much the world would change in the more than ten years since we published *"I just got a job in sales! Now what?"* I would have told them they were crazy. But change the world has. In 2003, the Internet was in full throttle. E-mail was the way of life. Anti-spam legislation and "do not call" lists were salespeople's biggest challenges. Twitter, Facebook, LinkedIn, and YouTube were barely on the radar. Texting was what high school and college students did.

Today, if you don't know the above terms, it's like you don't exist. Setting appointments rarely involves an actual phone conversation. If prospects formerly only read 50% of an e-mail, today they barely make it through the subject line. In even the most basic of sales, decision making involves a team who you may or may not actually need to interact with.

On the one hand, never has there been a more exciting time for salespeople. With yet another challenging economy, it's still the top profession where you control your own destiny. But challenges exist today that just weren't there 10 years ago. Relationships today have never been more important. With all the contact out there, everyone knows everyone—for better or worse. Everybody is connected to everyone.

Todd Natenberg is no exception.

Where do I begin to thank those who have helped in the past ten years of life? The superstar mentors who have paved the way for me - Brian Tracy, Tony Parinello, Stephan Schiffman and Roger

Dawson, I will always be grateful for your tutelage and support. We may not interact as often as we once did, but I still thank you for your amazing guidance.

For those amazing experiences and seminars I've had in my lifetime to walking on hot coals with Tony Robbins to studying on the beaches of Costa Rica with Dan Millman, I thank you for helping make me who I am today.

Managers from years gone by, like David Hackett, who I still keep in touch with, will always be friends. To current mentors like Aaron Brauch, thanks for believing in me.

For my best friend, Paul Rosen, who first got me into sales twenty years ago, loyalty still has your name on it.

For my family—my beautiful wife, Reena, and our amazing twin sons, Ari and Teddy- your inspiration is my inspiration.

Ten years ago, I said, "When you master the art of selling, you master the art of living." But recently a client challenged me. "Shouldn't it be the other way around?" she asked. "When you master the art of living, you master the art of selling."

With the love of Ari, Teddy and Reena, I am closer than I ever-thought possible. I truly am the luckiest man in the world.

Todd B. Natenberg
President, TBN Sales Solutions

Table of Contents

	Foreword	xiii
	Introduction	xvii
Chapter 1:	Set Goals	1
Chapter 2:	Schedule	13
Chapter 3:	State Initial Benefit	25
Chapter 4:	Prospect	41
Chapter 5:	Obtain Referrals	63
Chapter 6:	Build the Business Case	83
Chapter 7:	Follow Up	127
Chapter 8:	Overcome Objections	149
Chapter 9:	Network	167
Chapter 10:	Professional Development	187
	Conclusion	201

About the Author · 203

Additional Praise for TBN Sales Solutions… · · · · · · · · · · · 207

Also by Todd Natenberg · 211

Foreword

While negotiating is an integral part of what we do on a daily basis, there are few areas it is more important than in selling. But expert negotiators are not necessarily expert sales people. The two do go hand in hand, but to succeed in sales, much like succeeding in negotiating, salespeople needs a process. We've all heard the term "process" before, but rarely does a book come along that breaks it down to the microscope, as Todd Natenberg's *"I've been in sales for 10 years! Now what?"*

I've known Todd Natenberg for the past 10 years, since his first book, *"I just got a job in sales! Now what?"* was published in 2003. I have seen him progress as a sales expert and have noticed throughout, the success in the market from those who utilize his strategies. By revising his original book with updated techniques, tactics, scripts and formulas to coincide with the ever changing marketplace, Todd gives us a fresh approach that incorporates the proven fundamentals. He mixed the new with the old, the current with the proven. But unlike the thousands of other sales books on the market today, *"I've been in sales for 10 years! Now what?"* gives the proven professional tactics to take their business to the next level- that being of survival in today's market.

It is no big secret sales people burn out. While the rewards to succeeding in sales are spectacular, the pressures are just as tremendous. But veterans often get ignored when it comes to their slumps. Often, their managers used to work for them. So when it comes to the seasoned rep needing help, there are few avenues to go. Most managers will advise the veteran rep to "fix the problem," but won't tell them how.

Todd Natenberg- at long last- does. Written from someone who still lives the life, selling on a daily basis, *"I've been in sales for 10 years! Now what?"* will play an integral role in the selling industry for years to come.

Roger Dawson, Author of *Secrets of Power Negotiating*
Placentia, California

"When you master the art of selling, you master the art of living. Or is it when you master the art of living, you master the art of selling? Either way- to sell spectacular is to live spectacular. Be spectacular!"

Todd B. Natenberg

Introduction

John was in a rut. It was a rut he could not exit.
"Ten years!" he shouted to the sky one day. "I've been doing this for ten years. I don't need any help. I know what I'm doing. I was born to sell."

But John only was fooling himself. All he needed to do was look at his numbers. His first year in sales, he won President's Club, hit his quota twelve months straight, and ranked fifth out of 100 salespeople at the end of the year. He earned the MVP of his sales training course two weeks into the job. Five years ago, he rose to the rank of sales manager, where he supervised as many as twelve reps in two states. But management was not for him, and he happily returned to the trenches.

Newly married at the time with a first baby on the way, he welcomed less responsibility for more pay. Besides, he missed customer contact. At first, John picked up where he left off. Once again, he earned top commissions, won numerous awards, and mentored many of the younger reps. But these past three years things had changed. Each year, his ranking dropped. This past month, out of now two hundred reps, John numbered in the bottom twenty- 180 out of 200- rather than the other way around.

He couldn't figure it out. He was still the same person. His customers still liked him. He still had the positive mental attitude. His energy had never been better. He and his wife were living the American dream. She was a college professor who was six months pregnant with their second child. Financially, they were doing great.

John had wisely invested the money he had earned through real estate sales into stocks. But in terms of his professional fulfillment in sales, John was confused.

Steve, his sales manager, sat him down one day.

"John, we got a problem," Steve told him. "What is up with your numbers? You have not hit quota or even come close in the past six months. If I add up your numbers for the year, you are 30 percent of your target. What's going on with you? It's like you lost your mojo."

"I wish I knew," a dejected John said. "But you're right. I need to pick it up. Don't worry. I will."

"What can I do to help?" Steve answered.

"I don't think there's anything you can do," John replied. "I know it's up to me. Look, I still love this business. I'll fix it. You'll see."

"I hope so, John," Steve said directly. "Time is running out."

Running out? You mean I could go on probation—and potentially be let go? John thought. He had never been in this situation. The thought scared him beyond measure. But Steve was right. John had to change and change quickly.

But where to begin?

"I've been in sales for ten years!" John screamed to no one in particular in desperation. "Now what?"

What makes a great veteran salesperson? What separates salespeople who are regularly in President's Club from those who barely make ends meet? Is it luck? Is it hard work? Certain skills and attributes are necessary to thrive in sales, but succeeding over the long term goes well beyond developing simple tactics. Sales success involves applying those skills systematically and methodically to achieve a targeted objective. It means being consistent but continually evolving.

The success of a salesperson—rookie or veteran—comes down to one word: *process*.

Success involves understanding what it takes to succeed and then applying that process to what you plan to do. Sales are about sticking

INTRODUCTION

to a process—in good times and in bad. Football teams have playbooks. Basketball teams have offenses. The military has a war plan. If the great golfer Tiger Woods (back in his prime anyway) swings the exact same way every time from the tee box, the result would be a three hundred-yard shot down the middle of the fairway the overwhelming majority of the time. Selling is no different—for rookies or veterans.

To be the best of the best, you need a formula for success. Then, you need to follow that formula. The difference is that for you, the veteran, you have forgotten what made you tops in the first place. Whereas your goal was to become "unconsciously competent" (not having to think about what you already know), of late you have slipped into that level of "consciously competent" (thinking about what you need to do to be successful). Suddenly, it's not as easy to get back to that level you once took for granted.

The idea that you would have to return to the basics to, as sales manager Steve said, find your mojo may seem daunting. But if you did it once, you can – and will- do it again. You just need to recommit yourself, but in a different, improved way.

> *"One of the reasons mature people stop learning is that they become less and less willing to risk failure."*- **John Gardner**

So, what is the correct sales process for the seasoned pro? Selling comes down to embracing three critical philosophies:

Customers do not care how much you know until they know how much you care…but showing how much you care includes showing how much you care about YOURSELF.

Sell how you want to buy.

Selling is helping- pure and simple.

Over the next several pages, we will incorporate each of these philosophies into specific tactics in order return your business to the next level- and beyond.

I challenge you, my older Jedi warrior. Throw out what you think you know about sales. Clear your mind. Accept that the rookie salesperson has outperformed you for the last six months straight. But appreciate that you still control your destiny. You have the ability to change, to grow. That's what made you successful in the first place. You know how quickly you change your life? In a heartbeat.

THE 10-STEP SELLING PROCESS

1. Set Goals

2. Schedule

3. State initial benefit

4. Prospect

5. Obtain referrals

6. Build the business case (running a sales appointment)

7. Follow up

8. Overcome objections

9. Network

10. Professional development

CHAPTER 1

Set Goals

Goals: Everything you desire, deserve, and need to lead a balance, fulfilled life.

You can't get where you are going if you do not know where you want to be. If you do not know where you want to be, no roadmap will get you there.

Success comes from purpose. Until you recognize what makes you happy and why it does, you will lack motivation. Sales reps—your colleagues—burn out because they lose sight of the larger meaning. They forget that solving problems for others is honorable. They lack vision. They can't visualize the pot of gold at the end of the rainbow because they forget what the pot of gold looks like. What is your pot of gold? Why do you do what you do? Without the why, you will never enjoy what you do. Without the why, you will never fulfill your destiny.

In this chapter, we will present the playbook for setting goals:

1. What is your purpose in life?

2. SMART goals (Specific, Measurable, Attainable, Realistic, Time frame with deadline for professional and personal)

3. Visualize your goals

4. Celebrate your goals upon accomplishment

5. Continuously update your goals

1. What is your purpose in life?

What makes you happy? Do you know anymore? Ten years ago, life was simple. You wanted to make money to buy that fancy car, get that nice house, and take that fancy trip. Maybe you wanted to get promoted to sales manager. But now? Like John, you are a family man. It's not just about you anymore. Your goals and dreams are in direct proportion to your loved ones. But it's not just your life that has changed. The wants and needs of humanity have changed. Technology, for instance, has taken on a whole new meaning in the last decade. Have you adjusted? What does your perfect life look like today—and beyond? We must find out. Discovering your purpose comes in two steps:

    a. Realize what makes you happy.
    b. Create a vision.

> *Short term pleasure is about making money. Long term happiness is about serving others. When financial success is in direct proportion to how much you want to serve, that's fulfillment.*

Let's jump into the first exercise.

EXERCISE #G1—YOUR PURPOSE

Note: As you will see in a moment, despite the title of this exercise, you aren't going to just jump into the purpose. This is how you got into trouble in the first place. The sales process is not just about the ABC's, (always be closing) to quote the famous movie, Glengarry Glen Ross. Everything has a process within a process. So pay close attention, my friend).

    a. List 101 specific things you want in life, incorporating all aspects:

        1. Physical aspect (i.e., be a certain weight, complete a certain race)
        2. Community Aspect (i.e., be on a local board, volunteer for a charity)
        3. Spiritual aspect (i.e., meditation, attend church, attend synagogue)
        4. Relationships (i.e., go to your son's baseball game, go to dinner with your wife)
        5. Financial (i.e., take a $10,000 trip to London/Paris; make $100,000)
        6. Professional (i.e., sell 150 percent of quota, go to President's Club, be among top five salespeople at your company)

    b. Take no more than one hour.
    c. If you don't reach 101, that's okay, but don't go over the time limit. Remember, like the college test exams, your first answer is almost always the right one.
    d. Write it down.

    When you write something down, it becomes real. You can see it. You can touch it. It creates a life of its own. It holds you accountable. It holds the world accountable.

    e. Examine your list to determine underlying themes.

For instance, if several of the items that you want involve your family, one theme may be "serve my family." Or, if there appears to be a lot of spirituality, it may be "serve G-d." You decide.

    f. Take out a second blank sheet of paper and label it "My Purpose in Life."
    g. Write your purpose.

***"More men fail through lack of purpose than lack of talent."* – Billy Sunday**

See the following page for an example.

MY PURPOSE

The purpose of the life of Todd Natenberg is to create a world of contribution by serving as a loving role model for my amazing twin sons, Ari and Teddy, and my gorgeous wife Reena, to help others.

My incredible teaching talent, charisma, enthusiasm, playfulness, and zeal for living, have blessed me to achieve all I desire. I commit to long-term happiness, not short-term pleasure; a life of fulfillment, not shallow gratification; a life of peace, balance and service in which Ari and Teddy are proud to say, "That's my father. We are his sons."

2. **SMART goals (Specific, Measurable, Attainable, Realistic, Time frame with deadline for professional and personal)**

Enjoying what you do is important. Enjoying what you do because it enables you to lead the life you want is more important. For instance, it will be much easier to make a hundred cold calls if those hundred cold calls are necessary to achieve the income needed to achieve your goal of taking a $10,000 trip to London, Paris, and Rome. Or perhaps if your goal is to stay physically fit, realize that the reason you have that goal is that it will result in making you more alert, less irritable, and more productive. And if you are more productive, you will be able to make those hundred cold calls to achieve that income to buy that trip. It's a terrific never-ending circle.

If you asked former NBA star Michael Jordan at the height of his career if he enjoyed lifting weights, he might have said no. But because improving his overall fitness enabled him to be the best of the best, rarely would he miss a workout.

Now that you have a list of what you want in life, let's narrow our focus to written down specific personal goals, as they relate to your professional goals just as your professional goals relate to your personal goals.

> *"Everyone has a success mechanism and a failure mechanism. The failure mechanism goes off by itself. The success mechanism only goes off with a goal. Every time we write down and talk about a goal, we push the button to start the success mechanism."*
> – Charles "Tremendous" Jones, Motivational Speaker & Author

EXERCISE #G2—PERSONAL AND PROFESSIONAL GOALS

a. Get two blank sheets of paper
b. Label one "Personal Goals"
c. Label the second "Professional Goals"
d. Write down five personal goals for one month, six months, one year, and five years.
e. Write down five professional goals for one month, six months, one year, and five years.
f. Goals should be measurable, specific, and have the above deadlines.
g. When you have completed the exercise, you will have 40 total goals

- *Measurable*

The easiest way to understand measurable is being able to know when you have achieved your goal. For instance, "being happy" is not a goal, but "weighing two hundred pounds" is, because it's a concrete number. (Hey, just like sales!)

- *Specific*

Be as detailed as possible when writing down your goal. It's much more powerful to have a goal of taking a $20,000, one-month trip to London, Paris, and Rome and staying at five-star hotels rather than saying you would like to go to Europe.

On the professional side, if you might say your goal is to sell $50,000 within one year, a much better way to phrase it would read:

Sell $50,000 by obtaining three new accounts in Kansas City with a minimum size of $10,000 which will come from twenty new appointments and ten second appointments.

The more specific something is, the more real it is.
The more real it is, the more achievable it becomes.

- *Attainable/Realistic*

As much as you may want to play for the Chicago Cubs or Kansas City Royals, or even make $10 million dollars this year, is that truly attainable and realistic? Does your commission plan- even if you are 300% really make that possible? We are all for shooting for the stars and settling for the moon. But we can't shoot for a different galaxy. If you ask for something that is beyond a pipe dream, it will have the reverse effect and be extremely counterproductive. It will de motivate you, rather than inspire you.

- *Timeframe with deadline*

When are you the most productive? When do you get the most amount of work done in the least amount of time? It's always the day before you leave for vacation! Why? It's because you have no choice. You have no time to think. You just act. You have to focus, so nothing holds you back. You remove all obstacles because of the urgency. You know that if you don't achieve the goal, there will be consequences. The goal is not to scare you, but knowing consequences is motivation.

When I was a newspaper reporter at the *Daily Herald* in suburban Chicago, my best work always came under the most excruciating deadlines.

For instance, I will never forget this one time when I literally had five minutes to write a 500-word story. I was covering a village board meeting away from the newsroom. Laptop computers did not exist back then. I called my editor on a pay phone (Yes, it used to cost fifty cents to make a public call.) and literally dictated the story to him. I did this without even using a pen. I literally told the story. The article appeared the next day exactly as I "wrote" it.

> *"We should do this. We should do that. Until our shoulds become musts, we should all over ourselves."*
> – **Anthony Robbins**

3. Visualize your goals

Computers and hand-written notes help, but having a tangible object or picture to represent your goal is that much more powerful. Utilize something you can touch and feel.

When I first became a sales manager, I required my sales reps to write down their professional and personal goals. When the holidays came, I made their dreams a reality. I enabled them to see their goals.

For the rep who wanted to earn the money to buy a Porsche in one year, I bought a Porsche. For the rep who wanted a trip to France, I bought a trip to France. For the rep who wanted a camcorder, I bought a camcorder. What do you think I did?

The Porsche was a die-cast model Porsche. The trip to France was a puzzle of the Eiffel Tower. The camcorder was a key chain version of a View-Master. (Remember that toy we played with as kids? You looked into small binoculars to see cartoon photos.) Was it corny? Perhaps. But right up to the day I left, each rep had my gift proudly displayed on their desks.

Two years later, I even bumped into a rep on the streets of Chicago who I actually had fired due to lack of performance. Not only did he greet me warmly, he told me that to that day, he still has that Porsche model I gave him. Purpose is a powerful thing.

Determine the goal you want most and figure out how to visualize it. Buy the toy, put the photo on the wall.

> *There are three ways people learn, are motivated, and act upon: visual (what we see), audio (what we hear), and kinesthetic (feeling/movement). The act of selecting, seeing, and speaking a goal combines all three.*

4. Celebrate your goals upon accomplishment

Too often, people let life pass. They work to achieve, but when they do, they ask, "Is this all there is?" That's because they never enjoy the moments of success.

When you accomplish what you set out to do, be proud. Celebrate. Remind yourself that you accomplished your goal. The blood, the sweat, and the tears were worth it. If you won an award, post the plaque. If you received that $50,000 commission check, frame it. Of course, make sure you cash it first!

Have you ever heard the story of Hall of Fame Major League Baseball player Rickey Henderson? Legend has it that when he received his first $1 million paycheck from the Oakland Athletics, he was so proud that he did not cash it. True story.

> *If you don't know how success brings fulfillment, you will never want to repeat it. If you don't appreciate how it feels to be fulfilled, you will never seek it.*

5. Continuously Update Your Goals

You probably got into this mess because you took your eyes off the prize. When one prize is won, it's time for another. It's not that you aren't content with life, but human beings are programmed to always want and strive for more. Never-ending growth is what makes life fulfilling.

- Update your personal and professional goals yearly.
- Check off your goals each time you accomplish them.

So, what did we learn about goal setting?

1. What is your purpose in life?

2. SMART goals (Specific, Measurable, Attainable, Realistic, Time frame with deadline for professional and personal)

3. Visualize your goals

4. Celebrate your goals upon accomplishment

5. Continuously update your goals

When we stop growing, we stop looking forward to tomorrow. When we stop looking forward to tomorrow, we stop dreaming. When we stop dreaming, we stop living.

CHAPTER 2

Schedule

Time Management: A plan to execute your plan to achieve your goals.

Houses have foundations to build upon. Without a foundation, a house will collapse with the very first brick. The bricks may be adjusted systematically later, but the starting point of the foundation remains in place. Your bricks are your tasks. Your schedule is your foundation.

The best salespeople I know value their own time more than they value their prospects or customers. They fit others into their schedules, not the other way around. It's not arrogant. It's not condescending. It's smart business. Doctors, attorneys and accountants would never dream of moving their schedule around for you. Amazingly, you don't even expect them to, even though you are the client. What's the difference?

Helping others is not contingent on years of school, contrary to what society preaches. The difference is they view themselves as a consultant. Why don't you?

Since a typical day for a salesperson includes a variety of activities, it's important to manage your time wisely. In any given week, your responsibilities may include running appointments, sending follow-up letters, attending internal meetings, and prospecting.

Although tasks that do not involve client contact, such as writing proposals, can be completed after hours, work-life balance is important. Salespeople should not live and breathe work. The key to fitting essential tasks into regular work days is scheduling.

Time management is like writing an individual business plan. Outside factors may alter the plan, but it's critical there be a basis on which to operate. Earlier, we called it the foundation.

The difference this go around between you the veteran salesperson and you the 10 years ago rookie salesperson however is even more critical. You need to have your schedule- so then you can have the flexibility, when absolutely necessary, to alter it. But as we have certainly learned over the past 10 years, it is much less NECESSARY to alter it than we once thought.

In this chapter, we will present the playbook for managing your time:

1. **Recognize your daily, weekly, and monthly outcomes in your job**

2. **Create "Expect Excellence" with numeric measurements**

3. **Create your must work week**

4. **Cluster this must work week**

5. **Commit to your must work week**

> *"Obstacles are those frightful things you see when you take your eyes off your goals."* – Henry Ford

SCHEDULE

1. Recognize your daily, weekly, and monthly outcomes in your job

Busy and productive are very different. Busy creates stress. Productivity creates money, happiness and fulfillment. We can never be too productive.

Have you ever had a day where you worked hard but had nothing to show for it? Have you ever had one of those days where you felt you did absolutely nothing, but somehow eight hours had passed and it was time to go home? What do you do every day? What do you do every week? Do you even know anymore? Let's find out.

EXERCISE #S1—TRACK YOUR WEEK

a. Take out five sheets of paper.
b. Label each a day of the week (M–F).
c. Write on separate lines one-hour blocks from 8:00 a.m. to 5:00 p.m. (adjust accordingly if your hours differ).
d. For the next week, write down everything you do.- I mean everything.

This is not a list of what you *want* to do. This is what you actually *do*. Be honest. Honesty drives this exercise. Write down everything that occupies your time. Our goal is effective time management, not self-recrimination.

For instance, every time you check your voice mail, every time you dial a wrong number, every time you surf the Internet, write it down. I CHALLENGE you to separate yourself from the pack!

e. At the end of the week, tabulate all tasks into groups as there will be much repetition

f. Under each task, list the amount of time you dedicated that week to that task

g. Now ask yourself the simple question: "Did this task make me money?"

However you define making money is up to you. It may not have been a "closing appointment" or a "contract signing appointment." That's okay. But did it advance the sales process in a significant way that you can justify it – not to your manager- but yourself – and say that it indeed was necessary and productive?

 h. Where the answer to g is "Yes," put an A.
 i. Where the answer to g is "No," put a C.

Notice that we are removing the "B" from the traditional A, B, C goal setting exercise. That's because, at this stage of your career, either it's a "have to" get done, or "it doesn't really matter if it gets done." There simply is no in between.

For instance, if you think chatting with your colleague about plans for the weekend made you money because it put you in the right mindset, then include that as making you money.

Early in my sales career, I was a workaholic and a perfectionist. That got me nowhere. Sometimes you have to unwind. If that's what it takes to put you in the right mindset from time to time, go for it.

I recall fondly in my telecommunications days, a manager actually disciplined me for not "catching the football" that was thrown over my head by the top sales rep as I telemarketer.

"Geez, Todd, relax!" manager Mike told me. "It's great you work hard, but so do the other people, even though you may not believe it. That 10 minute football game enables them to make another 50 phone calls. Next time that football comes, I want you to throw it back at his head."

What's your formula for success?

> *"Few people think more than two or three times a year. I have made an international reputation by thinking once or twice a week."* **– George Bernard Shaw**

2. Create "Expect Excellence" with numeric measurements

Now that you know what makes you money on a regular basis, let's create a plan for those tasks. Only we are going to stop calling these tasks now. Let's replace that with the word "outcome."

Tasks sound like menial things performed to check off a list. That is what you tracked. But now that we determined which were effective, let's call them outcomes. Because outcomes lead to more outcomes to more outcomes. Hey, isn't that called the sales process?

Note: I realize we had you pick one week at random, and there may be other tasks that happen other weeks. If you think your week did not accurately reflect what you do, add tasks to your list of "tabulations." For instance, if there are monthly networking events or monthly sales meetings you must attend, include those tasks for the next exercise.

EXERCISE #SCH2—EXPECT EXCELLENCE

a. Write "Expect Excellence" at the top of a sheet of paper.
b. List your top 20 moneymaking outcomes from the previous exercise.

At the minimum, the list will include the following:

- Completed first appointments in person,
- Completed first appointments over the phone,
- Completed follow-up appointments in person,
- First time phone conversations with decision-makers

I will leave it up to you to come up with the other six tasks. Some other tasks may include sending follow-up e-mails, attending networking events, trade shows or even leaving voice mail. But this will vary depending on the type of sales you do.

For instance, when I had a true blue hunting positon in a local territory in telecommunications, pounding the phones or in person door knocking were effective outcomes. But as I progressed in my career to Discovery Education, where my role was part account management for growing accounts and part hunting, e-mail follow-ups sent to multiple decisions makers at one time, were vital to increasing my revenues.

Adjust your list accordingly, including that the week you selected may have neglected important other outcomes that are typical in a month or two months, just not the week you selected.

c. Next to each task, write down how many times you want to accomplish it weekly.

Even if your job is to sell $100,000 accounts to governments and school districts, as was my job as a district sales manager for Discovery, you will still have weekly goals, as I noted above.

SCHEDULE

> *"The outstanding leaders of every age are those who set up their own quotas and constantly exceed them."*
> – Thomas J. Watson, former chairman of IBM

    d. Create your must Expect Excellence

Now you know exactly what you want to accomplish. Let's determine how to do that now. It's time to put it all together.

I know, I know. You are not in a position to have a schedule. You have to be there for your customers. You must respond to every single call or e-mail immediately. But that simply is not true.

Look back at the week you just monitored. Did you spend the whole time responding to customer issues? How many were true emergencies? Customers and even hot prospects are much more reasonable than salespeople think. *You* might insist that they expect you to jump at their command, but they actually don't. They know what is an emergency to be addressed at the moment versus what is a problem that they just want to be kept in the loop on in the next twenty-four hours. Do you?

> *Just because a top customer calls, texts or e-mails you in a panic, they don't expect – or want- you to respond in a panic. Salespeople panic. Consultants resolve problems strategically.*

Remember, we are not being stubborn. We are only creating a foundation. Foundations may change. You may throw this whole schedule out the window, but I CHALLENGE you to give it a shot. It was the key to your success the first time. Try it again.

3. Create your must work week

Call this the "dream" scenario now. If you had 100% complete control over your schedule, when would you perform these outcomes? What days? What times?

> *"It is not enough to be busy; so are the ants. The question is, 'What are you busy about?'"* – Henry David Thoreau

EXERCISE #SCH3—CREATE YOUR MUST WORK WEEK

a. Once again, take out another five sheets of paper.
b. Once again, label each a day of the week (M–F).
c. Once again, write on separate lines one-hour blocks from 8:00 a.m. to 5:00 p.m. (adjust accordingly if your hours differ).
d. Insert your Expect Excellence outcomes.
e. Once you have the outcomes inserted, attach a numeric value to them for the week

Yes, this is the infamous when the manager asks you: "What are your numbers going to be this week?" This actually enables you to potentially answer! How many appointments do you want to run? How many phone calls do you want to make? How many e-mails do you want to send?

f. With the remaining hours that are still blank (if you have any that is), return to your A/C list to reexamine the C list.
g. Again, if there is still time in the week (and there may or may not be), see what in that C list – while not an A- may be more important than you thought and insert that in.

For instance, this may even include such health activities as working out, a networking meeting, or self-improvement class. Just a thought.

4. Cluster your must work week

Different tasks require different mindsets. Studies have shown that despite everybody being proud of multitasking, people get the most done when they focus on a particular task, then do it repeatedly over and over again. Have appointment days, prospecting times, e-mail times, etc.

> *Multitasking means you are ignoring something. If you try to do everything, you will accomplish nothing.*

Clustering also is important because it avoids you being a "star salesperson." Remember that term? It's the rep who meets in one part of the city, drives two hours to get to the other part, and then returns again to another part. That rep just spent six hours on three appointments. Top salespeople spend three hours on three appointments. Manage your time wisely.

5. Commit to your must work week

Now that you designed your plan, commit. Say it: "I commit to this schedule."

Look, my friend, we are not crazy here. Of course, you need some flexibility. If your entire week is closing appointments and it's the last week of the month, we don't expect you to cancel the appointments to prospect. But how often does that really happen? You just conducted some rigorous exercises. I applaud you.

Few rookie reps and even fewer superstar reps would take that time to self-examine. You are already in the elite. You are in the super super super star rep category. But don't forget who else does what we just did? Every CEO, Billionaire, Hall of Fame athlete coach, and leader of the free world.

> *Super successful salespeople have an executable plan. That plan is their schedule. They are the happiest because they control their lives. They don't let others control them. Which are you?*

Here are the top ways to commit to your must work week:

- *Never answer your cell phone (even though in this day, I'm sure it is your central point of contact)*

"But I have to answer the cell phone!" Really, says who? In this fast-paced environment, let me ask you about your own buying habits. Which upsets you more when you make a phone call as a buyer?:

Voice mail: *"Hi, you've reached Todd Natenberg. I'm not here right now. Please leave a message."*

Reaching salespeople - *"This is Todd. I can't talk right now. I have to go. Click."*

This goes back to what we said earlier about panic. Often when a client or prospect is calling you on your cell phone, they are upset. To quote my wife,

> *"Never argue with someone when they are upset."*
> **- Reena Natenberg**

- *Eat breakfast and lunch every day.*

Some people consider it a badge of honor to skip breakfast or lunch. That's absurd. This results in a lack of energy. The body needs physical nourishment. Food is fuel. Selling is a tough job both physically and emotionally. Eat. These meals affect your productivity the entire workday.

- *E-mail off-line.*

Although most non-money-making tasks should be done after hours, exceptions must be made. E-mail is one of those exceptions. E-mail is a tremendous resource. But do not get engaged in conversations on a computer screen. I will warn you. This is a very difficult rule to maintain- especially in the wake of today's Smart phones.

SCHEDULE

Customers will e-mail and text you like they're making a phone call. You have to be disciplined with this. If you find an "e-mail conversation" going on, pick up the phone for resolution. We will talk much more about this in later chapters

> *Salespeople should only use e-mail as a form of marketing, accountability, and clarification—not communication.*

By e-mailing offline, you will accomplish more in less time. Once in "e-mail mode," you can accomplish all your work without the distractions. Once you are done creating all your e-mails offline, connect online and send your mail.

- *Fill up your schedule to fit the week. Don't fill up your week to fit the schedule.*

When scheduling appointments, you pick the time (per your schedule). Tell prospects when you are available. Don't ask when they are available. If a prospect wants to meet on your "telemarketing" day, tell the prospect you are busy and pick a date and time that works for you.

Emergencies, such as customer service issues, will surface. Some issues will need to be addressed on the spot. Schedules will need to be altered. Don't become so tied to your schedule that there is no flexibility. But recognize what really is an emergency versus a situation when you are catering unnecessarily to someone else's needs at the expense of your own.

> *Ask yourself this question every time you are asked to readjust your schedule:*
>
> *If you were in front of a prospect closing a deal, if the prospect was signing the agreement then and there, would you leave the meeting? Would you answer the phone? Would you respond to e-mail? Would you stop*

> *doing what you are doing? If the answer is yes, then it is an emergency. If the answer is no, well, you know what to do.*

So, what did we learn about time management?

1. **Recognize your daily, weekly, and monthly tasks in your job**
2. **Create "Expect Excellence" with numeric measurements**
3. **Create your must work week**
4. **Cluster this must work week**
5. **Commit to your must work week**

> *It is only when we fear consequences that we truly commit to managing our time. When was the last time you missed an airplane—even with bad traffic?*

CHAPTER 3

State Initial Benefit

> Initial Benefit Statement: An explanation of what you are offering, who you are offering it to, and why anyone should care—in the exact opposite order.

If selling is helping, why wouldn't you share with prospects how you can help them? People can't be interested in you helping them if they don't what you can do to help.

Why should someone consider buying your product? Why should they take the time to hear you out, let alone meet with you? What are you offering? What makes it so good? If you don't believe in your product or your services, no one else will. But believing in what you offer goes beyond having a good mental mindset. Being able to articulate in a clear, concise manner is essential to succeeding in sales.

You must be able to state your initial benefit statement as a universal message. Having a scripted commercial explaining how you can help others from the onset is critical to your success. People talk about customizing your elevator pitch. This is incorrect.

> *Knowing where you are in the sales process it critical. Prospecting means you are talking to suspects- to convert them into prospects. Delivering the perfect scripted initial benefit statement is no different than*

doing an advertisement on television to the general masses. It's just cheaper.

If you were from Publisher's Clearing House and your job was to visit businesses to give checks for $1 million, would you ever change what you say? You would always say, "I'm Todd Natenberg. I'm with Publisher's Clearing House. You just won $1 million!"

In this chapter, we will present the playbook for stating the initial benefit.

1. **Know your ideal client**

2. **Know your features**

3. **Know your benefits**

4. **Write down your initial benefit statement**

5. **Understand how to use your initial benefit statement**

1. Know your ideal client

If you try to be everything to everybody, you will be nothing to nobody.

I will tell you who it is not. It is not "everybody." It's not "anybody who is open-minded to improving their business." Of course, you may sell to others outside your ideal target. But the idea here is that when you proactively prospect versus have leads come to you and ask for your services, you must know how to qualify your client. Before you can create your initial benefit statement, you must know who you think you can benefit the most.

If you don't know who you can help, then that person who you want to help will certainly have no idea you can help them.

Figuring out your ideal client can be challenging. To help, ask yourself certain questions about your existing best clients- or your company's. If you are a new company and have no existing clients, ask yourself certain questions about who you think would be your best client, if you had a magic wand. Here are the questions to ask about who you want to sell to:

a. How many employees does the company have?
b. What industry is the company in?
c. What is its annual revenue?
d. Is it publicly or privately traded?
e. How many locations does the company have?
f. How old is the company?
g. Where is it located? City? State? Zip code?
h. Where is its headquarters?
i. Is the company growing?
j. Is the company moving to new offices?
k. Did the company just move to a new office?

l. If your sale involves a company switching to your product, who does the company typically have prior to the switch)?
m. Who is the decision-maker? CEO? CFO? Controller? Owner?
n. What is the personality of the decision-maker?
o. Is it a man or a woman? What is the perfect age of the decision maker?
p. Is the decision-maker on LinkedIn?
q. What industry are they in?
r. Do they sell a tangible product (equipment) or intangible (services)?

The ideal client has those characteristics you can find through means other than asking people. In other words, if you wanted to find your ideal client, you could create a list merely by scouring the Internet or going to the local library. If your list requires interviewing others, this is not an ideal client

Who is the ideal client for TBN Sales Solutions?

Fifty to five hundred employees
10 to 100 salespeople
$5 million–$100 million in annual revenues
Outside salespeople who call on accounts in person
Base salary of $40,000 + $100,000 with commissions
Base salary of $50,000 + $85,000 with bonuses
Monthly, quarterly quotas or annual targets
Multiple locations with headquarters in a major city
Salespeople have never had formal sales training
Company is at least ten years old
Decision maker is VP of Sales/CEO
Technology company
Telecommunications company
Printers/web designers/graphics company
Realtors (100 percent commissions)
Mortgage Brokers (100 percent commissions)
Financial Planners (100 percent commission)
Insurance Agents (100 percent commission)
Network marketers (100% commission)
One-person entrepreneurs

EXERCISE #SIB1—WHO IS YOUR IDEAL CLIENT?

a. Take out a sheet of paper and label it, "Who is my ideal client?"
b. Examine the last five customers you or your company sold.
c. Write down the top twenty characteristics of each customer.
d. Compare your results of all five customers.
e. Write the 20 most common measurable characteristic.
f. Set aside document for now (we will return to it later).

2. Know your features

Before you can properly state your initial benefit, identify what you have in your arsenal. Everybody says they know the difference between features and benefits. But do you really?

> *Features are indisputable facts, what you actually provide, not how they can help your client. But while you want to tell prospects how you can help them, they do need to understand the features you offer to understand how you will implement that strategy.*

If you sell cellular phone service, features include texting, free long distance, online billing, and twenty-four-hour customer service. If you sell copiers or other tangible equipment, the various models, warranties, and leasing options are features. Twenty-four-hour service may sound like a benefit, but it's just a feature. It's merely a service you offer.

Specifics about your company also are features. If your company is 50 years old and has 100 employees with 20 customer service people, being 50 years old, having 100 employees and 20 customer service people are all *features*.

EXERCISE #SIB2—What Are Your Features?

a. Take out a sheet of paper and label it, "What are my features?"
b. List your top 10 features of the products you offer.
c. If you have multiple products, pick top 5 products and list 10 features of each
d. List your top 10 features of the company you work for
e. List your top 10 features of yourself

WHAT ARE THE FEATURES OF TBN SALES SOLUTIONS?

Todd B. Natenberg- Personal

1. Author of *"I just got a job in sales! Now what?"*
2. Author of *"I've been in sales for 10 years! Now what?"*
3. 20 years' experience as sales manager/sales trainer/salesperson
4. Former daily newspaper reporter
5. Former business newspaper reporter
6. 141-mile Ironman Triathlon finisher in 16 hours 30 minutes
7. Adventurer (hang gliding, sky diving, bungee jumping)
8. Volunteer on Kibbutz (communal living) in Israel
9. Author of *The Journey Within: Two Months on Kibbutz*
10. Volunteer coach for basketball/baseball for twin sons teams
11. Membership committee of local synagogue
12. Married to Canadian college professor of piano, Reena Natenberg
13. Father of fraternal twin sons, Ari and Teddy Natenberg

TBN Sales Solutions- Professional

14. ½ day – weeklong customized private workshops
15. "How to Double Your Productivity in ½ the Time workshop
16. "How to Double Your Prospects in ½ the Time" workshop
17. "How to Skyrockets Other Sales; How they will skyrocket yours" workshop
18. "How to Triple Your Sales without Hiring a Soul" workshop
19. "The Lure of Leadership" workshop
20. "How to Double Your Sales in ½ the Time" workshop
21. One on one 9-week customized sales course
22. Follow up ongoing coaching via e-mail
23. One-on-one ongoing sales consulting with retainer
24. Keynote speaking for associations
25. "I just got a job in sales! Now what?" keynote

26. "Bad economy? Sell your way out of it!" keynote
27. "No more cancellations!" keynote
28. "Why won't they call me back?" keynote/workshop
29. Ridealongs via phone or in person
30. Written customized sales business plans
31. Electronic/printed handouts with seminars
32. Customized scripts

3. Know your benefits

Now that you know what you offer, you need to explain why people should care.

> *Benefits are the positive, tangible impact those features have on your ideal client to enhance their business.*

People say benefits are overrated. That is not true. When you are talking to your ideal client, the words you pick will trigger interest, if you truly know your ideal client.

I recently heard a colleague in my profession say benefits like "impact the bottom line" and "improve productivity" are old school. If that's how your clients talk, it isn't. Talk their language. It's not about you. It's about them. How do they speak? When they hear their lingo, they pay more attention—whether they admit it.

I recently attended a networking event and spoke with a salesperson for a financial planning firm. I did not know at the time what he did, but here's what I said when he asked what I do:

"I'm the president of TBN Sales Solutions. We increase commissions for salespeople through customized training. We establish step-by-step processes with private workshops, individual consulting, and keynote speaking for associations to impact the bottom line."

He literally cut me off after the word "training." He was in sales. He made commissions. He wanted to be more productive. Those were his triggers.

"You need to call my owner," Paul told me. "He'd love to talk to you."

The most common benefits are:

- Increase revenue
- Impact the bottom line

- Improve productivity
- Enhance efficiency
- Reduce costs
- Improve the quality of life

EXERCISE #SIB3—What Are the Benefits of Your Offering?

    a. Take a sheet of paper and label it, "What are my benefits?"
    b. Return to those top ten features.
    c. Write the top ten benefits of those features.

4. Write down your initial benefit statement

It's time to write your initial benefit statement. Your statement should be two sentences. One is too short. Three is too long. Two is ideal.

Sentence one should have benefit with features targeting the most important aspect of your ideal client. Sentence two should be more specific features ending with benefits.

Why is it so critical a benefit statement include features and benefits? Again, go back to your own buying habits.

Have you ever spoken with someone who talks only in benefits? A negative stereotype might be a poor network marketer. Right? Here's how that conversation may go:

    Buyer: "What do you do?"
    Seller: "I help make people money."
    Buyer: "How do you do that?"
    Seller: "I just do. If you meet with me for 20 minutes, I can explain."

    How annoying is that?

Now, who speaks often in features? A negative stereotype might be a poor car salesperson. Right? All they do is list everything under the sun, whether you want to hear it or not.

Note: I do not mean to pick on network marketers or car salespeople. I know many fantastic ones and they are my clients. Let me emphasize when I say these are the bad ones.

In writing your initial benefit statement, look to elicit the "no kidding!" response. This is named in honor of my former editor, Mark Shepherd, at the *Columbia Missourian* during my journalism days. "Shep" said that when reading the first two sentences of a story, known as a lead—in essence an initial benefit statement—readers should say, "No kidding!" They should want to read more.

For instance, our statement as noted above at TBN Sales Solutions:

"I'm the president of TBN Sales Solutions. We increase commissions for salespeople through customized training. We establish step-by-step processes with private workshops, individual consulting, and keynote speaking for associations to impact the bottom line."

So in my statement, what are the features? What are the benefits? Who is my ideal client?

Our features are customized training, step-by-step sales processes, private workshops, individual consulting, and keynote speaking. Our benefits are to increase productivity and impact the bottom line. My ideal clients are salespeople, individuals and associations. Make sense?

Yes, even customized training is a feature. It's a specific feature, but a feature nonetheless. There are public trainings, and then there are customized trainings. Mine is customized. Our ideal clients are salespeople.

5. Understand how to use your initial benefit statement

As stated earlier, this statement is never customized. I repeat: it is *never* customized. This does not mean you won't add words to your *pitch*. Your pitch and your initial benefit statement are different.

> *Pitching your services is a response to when people ask you about your initial benefit statement. You pitch prospects. You give an initial benefit statement to suspects. There is a difference.*

So when to use it?

- In your e-mail signature to reflect what you do
- On your signature for your Smartphone
- At all networking events when people ask what you do
- Any informal time when people ask what you do
- In every first voice mail message to a prospect.

> *Give people a reason to call you back, and they will. For all you know, they could be interested. If Sprint cellular left you a voice mail five minutes after you had a problem with AT&T, would you call them back? Only if you knew why they were calling.*

We will talk more about this in the prospecting chapter, but for now, here's an example:

"This is Todd Natenberg, President, TBN Sales Solutions, (816) 876-9184. I'm calling to see if we can help. We increase commissions for salespeople through customized training. We establish step-by-step processes with private workshops, individual consulting, and keynote speaking for associations to impact the bottom line." I want to see if we could help. Again, Todd Natenberg, TBN Sales Solutions, (816) 876-9184.

> *Being wordy means you are rambling. Leaving a clear, direct and effective message, even if it lengthy is being professional.*

When someone calls you back based on this message, you know they are interested. If they don't call you back, at least you know they know what you do and what you offer.

- Any time you are trying to get an appointment with the decision-maker, even if you are sure you are not speaking to the person in charge.

We will delve more on this in the next chapter. Suffice to say, for now, you never know who you are speaking to, so treat everyone like they are the person in charge.

So what did we learn about the initial benefit statement?

1. Know your ideal client

2. Know your features

3. Know your benefits

4. Write down your initial benefit statement

5. Understand how to use your initial benefit statement

> *If someone finds your effective complete initial benefit statement wordy or too long, who cares? They weren't who you were trying to help anyway.*

CHAPTER 4

Prospect

> Prospecting: Uncovering qualified opportunities through various methods to advance potential clients in the sales process.

Prospecting is like making new friends, meeting strangers for the first time, or the first date. The anticipation can be exciting and scary. But the results can be spectacular.

Without prospects, your selling skills are worthless. As a veteran, you may prospect differently than you once did, but you still must prospect to return to your status as top salesperson. Top dogs never forget the importance of prospecting. They realize the sales process does not only relate to the sales appointment.

To prospect effectively, remember what prospecting is all about and what it is not. Of all the steps in the process, none are more important than prospecting. It's your lifeline.

In this next chapter, we will present the playbook for prospecting:

1. **Prepare**

2. **Ways to prospect**

3. **There are no gatekeepers**

4. State initial benefit

5. Empower who you are speaking to

6. Ask for appointment

7. Confirm verbally

8. Send Outlook Invite

1. Prepare

Effective prospecting is a mindset. You need to understand what you want to accomplish, why you want to accomplish it, and how to accomplish it. The best salespeople do not view prospecting as drudgery. They view it as a means to an end.

Everyone and every company are not prospects. They are "suspects." They might *become* a prospect, but not until certain criteria are revealed, such as their timeframe, whether solutions can be provided to meet their needs, and whether they have sufficient resources. The good news is in today's digital age, suspects can become prospects much quicker. The bad news is it that it takes even more to get prospects to become clients.

That's why with Facebook, LinkedIn, Twitter, and whatever social media you choose, expertise in this step is more important than ever. You will only get one chance to turn that suspect to a prospect, so be ready.

- *Set a firm date and time each week to prospect.*

You have already outlined what days and times you will prospect. Now, it's time to execute. As we said, you would never cancel an appointment with someone who may buy your service. Treat the time you prospect no differently. Discipline is key.

Think back to how you got into this situation of poor performance. Wasn't it that your prospects somehow ran out? You probably are at the point in your career where you think you worked solely on referrals. Am I right? You simply didn't have time to prospect anymore. Clients called you. But at some point, the well went dry. The funnel went blank. Now, it's time- urgent time- to get that funnel back up.

But remember once we fix this, let's keep it fixed.

Appointments with yourself to prospect must be just as firm as appointments with customers willing to buy. It's worth repeating: "Would you ever cancel one appointment for another if one of those appointment were signing a contract?"

- *Leave your desk when making phone calls (call from conference room, if you can).*

Desks are distractions for even the most organized salesperson because they remind us of all the things we have to do.

- *Forward voice mail/turn off your cell phone/don't connect to the Internet.*

Voice mail, cell phones, e-mail, and the Internet are effective sales tools when utilized properly. However, when you prospect, none of these mechanisms should be operational. If you use an account management tool, such as Salesforce.com, Siebel, or even Outlook, make sure you use these databases offline. This will eliminate any temptation to respond to e-mail or surf the Internet. All research should be done before you prospect.

Regarding cell phones, never prospect from cell phones in the field. The issue isn't the potential static on the line with your customer. Often cell phones are just as clear as landlines. No, you need your computer screen open to take notes, schedule the appointment on the spot, and just overall be alert to the conversation, if you actually reach someone. If you are using a cell phone as a landline and you are in your office environment, of course, that is the exception.

- *Stand up when you make phone calls.*

Physically, your voice sounds more imposing when you stand. When you talk leaning back in a relaxed position, your voice is more sluggish. Also, standing during a phone call keeps you more alert.

- *Smile into a mirror.*

People can tell when you smile on a phone call. It's like standing. You are more effective and more pleasant. A mirror will remind you to smile. Prospecting also can be lonely. When you look into a mirror, you have a friend—you.

- *Don't hunt for elephants during prospecting time.*

It's important you don't spend your time on opportunities that will not make you or your company money. However, nothing is more dangerous than going to the other extreme and only looking for the "big one." Large deals are defined as those that are at least three times your monthly quota. It's good to have these in the funnel, but realize that they take much longer to close and are much more work.

Salespeople who spend all their time searching for elephants tend to perform erratically. Their monthly numbers are up and down, and they jump from company to company. Consistent reps are much more valuable. Would you rather have one huge deal every six months and no sales in between or five consecutive months of midsized deals that are worth more overall?

> *"It is better to sell a large number of cars at a reasonably small margin than to sell fewer at a large margin of profit. It enables a large number of people to buy and enjoy (the car) and gives a large number of men employment at good wages. Those are two aims I have in life."* – **Henry Ford**

- *Have fun!*

Some reps like prospecting more than others, but few love it. Prospecting is a means to an end. When you realize how much closer prospecting brings you to that big commission check, you will like it more. But there are things you can do in the interim to make it more tolerable. Start by having fun. Make a game of it.

Pair up with a partner at the office. Bet colleagues how many buildings you can get thrown out of or how many people will hang up on you.

> *"Opportunities are usually disguised as hard work, so most people don't recognize them."* **– Anne Landers**

- Refuse rejection

When people treat you rudely, 99 percent of the time, the reasons have nothing to do with you. The odds are they are having a bad day, something bad just happened, or they are angry at the world. People who take out aggressions on innocent salespeople are insecure and bitter. They have nothing better to do than to be mean to strangers. Laugh at them. Pity them. Don't get upset. Why waste the energy?

> *People refusing to hear your ideas and people rejecting you are two very different things. Close friends and families reject. Prospects refuse. Recognize the difference.*

One day, early in my career, I cold-called a company in person. Wearing a suit and tie and carrying a briefcase, I was clearly the salesperson. But before I could even say, "Hello, my name is…" the woman at the front desk interrupted. She ordered me to leave and threatened to call security. Perplexed, but recognizing my presence was not the reason for the outburst, I decided to turn my negative experience into an opportunity to break the ice with my next encounter at another business.

"Hello, my name is Todd, and I'm with USN Communications," I told my next opportunity. "Please don't yell at me. I just left a potential customer downstairs who almost took my briefcase and threw it at me before I could even get two words in."

The woman at the front laughed. Then she responded, "Really? That didn't happen to be XXX Company, did it?"

"Yes," I replied with a smile. "As a matter of fact, it was. Do you know the woman?"

"No," she responded. "But I do know they were robbed at gunpoint two days ago by a stranger claiming to be a salesperson."

> *Always ask yourself when you assume the worst in people, "What else could this mean?"*

- *Establish numeric maximum and minimum goals.*

Have goals for your prospecting time. Your maximum goal should be nothing short of making the sale on every call. On a more realistic level, set numeric goals. For instance, you may want to make 50 phone calls, reach 10 decision-makers, have 10 hang-ups by secretaries, leave 20 voice mails, have five conversations with decision-makers, and schedule five appointments. Don't limit the goals to how many phone calls you make and how many appointments you schedule. Go back to your "Expect Excellence" list.

- *Track your numbers.*

We discovered earlier that the reason Tiger Woods succeeded back in the day is that he had a formula. So why is not doing as well today? The same theory applies in that he has gone away from his formula. We know a big part of his regression is his mental state. But if experts dissected his swing, they would clearly see his process is different every time now. You can do the same- that is being the first Tiger Woods! Record your numbers every day. Don't do it for your sales manager. Do it so you can monitor your own progress.

> *The quicker you know what success is, the more you can repeat it. The more you can repeat it, the easier it is.*

Understand how many phone calls you need to make to reach a decision-maker, how many times you need to have a decision-maker hang up on you to schedule an appointment, and of course how many appointments to close a deal.

When you know your ratios, your job is easier and much more pleasant. Analyze your progression every time you prospect. By tracking your numbers, you determine how many phone calls you need to make to reach how many live decision-makers.

Tracking your numbers should cover the four main areas of prospecting:

Phone calls, e-mails, in-person visits, and networking events.

> *The best salespeople I know judge their success in prospecting by the amount of refusals they receive rather than the amount of appointments they schedule. They literally prospecting for the nos. It tells them they are doing well.*

The following page is a daily tracker. Copy and use it every time you prospect. It will serve as a manager when you have no manager. When properly used, this is a remarkable tool. If you want to add categories, feel free, but do not delete what is written. This document gives you an honest assessment.

As you finish calls, enter numeric slashes under the appropriate category. At the end of the day, the tracker will allow you to easily summarize your prospecting successes and track the events that lead to each success.

> *Accept the fact that 80 percent of your phone calls will result in voice mail, 10 percent will result in conversations with someone who you think is NOT the decision-maker, and only 10 percent will result in speaking with who you think you want to.*

PROSPECT

DAILY TRACKER

Date of prospecting

Appointments scheduled

Sit-down conversation with decision-maker, with follow-up appointment scheduled

Hot interest from decision-maker after five-minute talk—90-day follow-up plan (no firm appointment, but good talk)

Blow-off by decision-maker (hang-up, don't ever call me again)

Left voice mail on direct line of decision-maker

Nice conversations with secretaries and left voice mail

Blow-offs by "gatekeepers" (gave a business card, got a card, hung up by secretary, not transferred to voice mail)

Information gathered from secretary to utilize in speaking to decision-maker

Phone calls returned after messages left

Wrong #

411 call

Checked my own voice mail

Referrals obtained

©2015, Todd Natenberg
TBN Sales Solutions, (816) 876-9184, www.ijustgotajobinsales.com

- *Have everything you need to close the sale with you or in front of you.*

Your optimal goal always is to close a sale. If you are selling big-ticket items, the odds are lower, but you never know.

> *"It is better to be prepared for an opportunity and not have one than to have an opportunity and not be prepared."* – **Whitney Young, Jr.**

If you are door-knocking, be as prepared as you would be if you were conducting a scheduled appointment. Have contracts, pricing, date book, etc. with you on the initial call (see the following page for a checklist). If you are telemarketing, have everything you would have if the person on the other end were sitting across from you live. Be organized. Don't ever be in a position where you have to call back potential customers because you don't have information that you left at the office.

Everything I Need to Have When I Prospect

- Pen
- Pad of paper for notes
- Datebook
- Business cards
- Pricing (all pricing)
- Contracts (necessary documents requiring signatures)
- Internal paperwork (demonstrating to customers what's required on your end)
- Product samples (either physical or pictures)
- Presentations (electronic or written)
- Testimonial letters about your company
- Testimonial letters about you
- Media articles about your company
- Media articles about your company's industry
- Color brochures about your company

- Color brochures about your product
- Written guarantees your company or product offers
- Contact information (phone/e-mail) for internal resources to call on the spot
- Implementation procedure form to handout (one pager)
- "What Your Company Can Do for You" (one pager)
- Company contacts (one pager)
- Personal profile (one pager)

2. Ways to prospect

There are various ways to prospect. All are effective in various capacities. What works for you? Do you tele market? Will you make in-person cold calls? Will you scan newspapers? Will you network?

The following is a list of various resources and techniques for earning new clients, as well as suggested introductions for each.

- Customers
- Friends/relatives (Is there anyone who wants to help you more?)
- Door-knocking (unannounced in-person visits)
- Telemarketing (unannounced phone calls)
- Territory by city, state, or zip code
- Target a particular industry (vertical marketing)
- Target a company size (by revenue or number of employees, etc.)
- Library databases (such as Sorkin's)
- Customer lists of competitors (if you can somehow get a list of them)
- Social media (LinkedIn, Facebook, Twitter)
- Vendors of yours (who you buy from)

Anybody you do business with, including your accountant, attorney, insurance agent, web designer, local phone provider, long distance phone provider, cell phone provider, office equipment provider, health club, landlord/condo association, barber, grocery store manager, dry cleaner and more you should ask them for their business.

The rule is simple: If you pay them for their services, they should at least consider paying you for yours.

- Media articles about companies or "movers/shakers" ("I'm calling in response to the article about you in…I wanted to congratulate you. We work with companies like yours…")

- Members of associations in which you or your company have memberships
- Members of chambers of commerce in which you or your company have memberships
- Members of chambers of commerce in the area in which you live or your company is located (even without membership)
- Alumni of high school or college

3. There are no gatekeepers

What is a gatekeeper? According to *Merriam-Webster's* dictionary, a "gatekeeper" is…wait a second. It's not listed in the dictionary. Exactly.

In the old days of selling, they taught: "Never take no from someone who can't say yes." That was fine 50 years ago, but today the problem with this philosophy is that you don't know for certain that the person you are speaking with is not authorized to buy. At the minimum, you don't know that they are merely a "secretary."

Add to that the fact that, in today's market, even if a true decision-maker is at their desk when you call, they aren't going to answer the phone. That is, they won't answer the phone, unless of course someone tells them it's worth it.

It's safe to say that the person answering phones up front is used to one of two greetings by salespeople: They either charm the greeter to death to get the "person in charge" or they completely ignore and disrespect the person upfront to barrel through to the person in charge.

But what if they are the person in charge? Imagine this conversation:

Salesperson: "Can I speak to the person in charge?"

Counter person: "I am the person in charge! What? You think because I sit at the front counter, I have no responsibility?"

Once, when I was a sales manager, a sales rep and I knocked on doors. We approached a company, and the secretary greeted us. Rather than barreling her over asking for the decision-maker, we stated our initial benefit. Before she could respond, a man approached.

He indicated he had overheard our pitch. "Phone service? Did you say phone service? Your timing is very good," he said. "But I missed the beginning of what you said. What exactly do you do?"

We stated our initial benefit statement again. Another man approached. He, too, had overheard the conversation. "Phone service? Did you say phone service? Our Internet is down as we speak," he commented. Two weeks later, we signed the deal.

And two years after that, Technomic International, Inc., in Northbrook, Illinois, became the first TBN Sales Solutions client.

Another important note to emphasize on "there are no gatekeepers" is that with today's fast paced technology having evolved 100 fold since the original *"I just got a job in sales! Now what?"* was published, true decision makes often are not the same people who sign on the dotted line.

Did you ever see *The Wizard of Oz?* Do you remember when Dorothy couldn't get in to see the wizard? A literal gatekeeper wearing a green funny hat and mustache yelled, "Nobody see the wizard!" He then slammed the door on her.

But then Dorothy started to cry with her friends comforting her. The man in the funny hat watched and when he heard her talk about Auntie Emm, the man opened the door.

"I can't take it," he said, himself crying. "I have an Auntie Emm too. Come on in. I'll get you to the wizard."

> *They used to say don't take no from someone who can't say yes, but realize when prospecting that person who you think can only say no knows what it takes to get to that person who can say yes.*

Here's a process to differentiate you:

- *Humanization*

The first thing you ask either the person you see or who answers the phone is their name. The sound of a person's name is the sweetest sounding name to that person. Then use the name in the conversation.

If they won't tell you, don't push it. But I guarantee that more than 50 percent of their time, they will tell you. The key is to ask it immediately, before a wall goes up and they get tired of answering all your questions

- *Ask for help with the exact word "help"*

   Everyone wants to help and get help to and from professional consultants. No one wants to talk to salespeople.

- *Explain why you picked this particular company (even on a cold call)*

Everyone wants to be chosen. No one wants to be called upon just because you are cold-calling. Even if you actually are cold-calling, there's a reason you found this organization. Maybe it is its location, the type of industry, or the company size. Tell prospects *why* you chose them.

   Nothing is a cold call. Everybody you pick is for a reason. Maybe they are in your territory. Maybe they meet your "small and mid-sized" business criteria. Maybe they were a true personal referral. You would never call up somebody and tell them, "I picked you out of the hat. I don't know a thing about you." Remind your prospects of this.

Companies are like individuals. They want to be acknowledged for their unique characteristics. No one wants to be picked at random.

4. State your initial benefit

This is the kicker. Salespeople in the past may have asked people up front for their name and then for help. But how many have given that person the respect of stating their initial benefit. End it with, "I wanted to see if that is something you and your company would be interested in exploring."

Never come down to people's levels. Come up.

Here are some terrific icebreakers for prospecting:

- **"Hello. How are you? Oh, all right. I know that look. You're thinking, 'Quick, head for the hills. Here comes the salesperson. Act busy.'"**

- **"All right, I surrender. I admit it. I'm a salesperson. Shoot me dead in my tracks now and get it over with."**

- **"Hello, how are you? Look, do me a favor and just talk to me. This is the tenth call I've made in the last hour. I've been hung up on ten times and had my brochure ripped up ten times. It's been a long day!"**

- **"Can I have a cheeseburger and fries?"** (Say this if they have a sliding glass window up front.)

- **"Oh, So-and-So is not here now? He probably knew I was coming and ran away."**

(If they do not laugh at all at any of these jokes): **"Oh, come on. That was a little funny, don't you think?"**

- **"Hi, what's your name? Nice to meet you, so and so. I'm Todd Natenberg. The reason I'm calling you is...."**

(We are allowed to be upfront, you know).

5. Empower

Let's assume that you have done all that we have suggested and the people upfront have indicated that they truly have no authority to decide whether to purchase your services. Don't let them have that easy way out. Give them the power. As noted above, they will appreciate it.

Here's how it might work:

You: "So, prospect So and So. Can we schedule an appointment with yourself and whoever else also is involved in the buying process to see how we can help?"

Buyer: "Oh, you are very nice. But as I said, I'm not the person to speak to. I'm just a receptionist."

You: "While I appreciate that, So and So. That's not entirely true. You are very important to the company. You are the face of the company greeting me and others. Do you handle that person's schedule? What can you and I do together to facilitate a meeting? Do you think that person would be interested in our services? Thanks so much for your help."

Other great questions to ask the receptionist include, "What would it take for that person who does make the decisions to be interested in our services? When was their last new purchase?"

> *There are decision makers, signers and allies. With the fast paced environment we live, allies are just as important as the decision maker. They don't say yes, but they know what it takes to get a yes.*

A great example is that for my first book, one of my top endorsements (whose name I will not reveal to protect the innocent) came from this very strategy. Here's what happened:

When I called up and sent my manuscript, a woman answered the phone. I treated her just like she was who I wanted to endorse my book. She was very nice and appreciated my very unique approach to treating her like she truly was the person in charge and not just the secretary. After even going so far as beyond up above, I asked for her direct name and direct e-mail. Guess who it was? The owner's wife!

Enough said.

6. Ask for appointment

If you finally reach the person with whom you want to speak, close for an appointment right there. While you are a top-notch consultant, it still remains that you intruded. It was not scheduled. If prospects are ready to meet on the spot, that's great. However, be aware that being ready to meet and giving you five minutes to hear what you have to say are two different things.

> *Prospecting is not about prospects hearing what you have to say. It's about discovering their needs to determine whether you can help.*

Here are some basic dos and don'ts when it comes to scheduling appointments:

- *Never conduct an appointment standing up.*

It's a negative sign if prospects are not willing to physically sit down with you in a meeting, even if they say they are interested.

"This is fine," they might say. "Let's chat right here."

Don't do it.

Your job is to generate enough interest to create an opportunity. Opportunities only happen when both parties are willing to sit down to engage in a conversation. A good measure is to never stand up chatting more than five minutes.

If the prospect appears interested, then ask permission to continue at that moment. Say, "I know I came by unannounced, but it sounds like we may be in a position to help your company. Do you have at least a half hour to chat right now? If not, let's schedule an appointment."

If they agree, they will automatically invite you into their office or a conference room. Congratulations! You just shortened the sales cycle. If they indicate they don't have the time, then schedule a future appointment at that precise moment. Here's a recommended script:

"I'm glad you're interested, So-and-So. But this information is very important, and I don't want to review it by the seat of our pants. I'd be wasting your time and my own. They are equally valuable. Let's schedule something. How's Thursday at 9 a.m.?"

The only time it is acceptable to have that standup meeting is if you are calling on an existing client, who has already paid for your services in the past. If they are standing and want to chat, then it's okay. You have a special relationship with them that puts you beyond the prospecting step. But be selective with this strategy, even with paying clients.

- *Schedule the appointment at that moment.*

Don't say that you'll call next week to schedule an appointment. Do it right there, even if it's a tentative appointment. Pull out your date book. Suggest a date and time based on your schedule. You asked to meet, so you should decide when. If the prospect can't meet on your terms, compromise.

- *Qualify.*

Some salespeople erroneously believe that once you schedule the appointment, you should leave right away. They fear prospects will change their minds.

> *Prospects that change their minds about meeting with you do so because they were never interested in the first place.*

Make sure prospects meet *your* criteria. Go back to your ideal client. Are there enough characteristics that they qualify? If prospects have no intention of switching phone providers for two years, for instance, don't schedule a meeting now.

An introductory meeting might be beneficial, because if the prospect's situation changes, you want to be the first person the prospect thinks of to contact. But be smart.

Another reason why it's important to qualify is that sometimes prospects will meet with you knowing they have no intentions of utilizing your services. They only do so because they want to obtain pricing information from your company to use as leverage against their current vendor. Their goal is for their current vendors to lower their prices—at your expense.

A good example of these kinds of prospects is ones who have stiff penalties if they switch providers. It's important to ask these prospects point blank, "I'm confused. If you would incur a $1 million penalty by switching away from your current vendor, and you only spend $3,000 per month, what's the purpose of meeting? I know I wouldn't switch if I were you…unless there's more to the issue."

> **Buyers are not liars—when you ask the right questions.**
>
> *"Never complain about what you permit."*
> **– Mike Murdock**

- *What is the role of the individual?*

Ask before you finish the call, "I'm excited to meet with you, but just to make sure we are all on the same page, walk me through the buying process. Who signs on the dotted line? Is that you?"

You still may meet, even if your prospect is not the decision-maker, but you must identify that. If the process goes through this individual, you keep the meeting. But finding that out is critical.

Don't waste your time or the prospect's. They are equally valuable.

7. Confirm verbally.

There are two schools of thought about confirming meetings. One says to never confirm, because you give the prospect a chance to cancel. The other says to always confirm because your time is valuable. Do confirm appointments, but do it in a way that empowers YOU!

Say this:

"I'll tell you what, So-and-So. Here's what I'll do next week. The day before our appointment, by noon at the latest, I will send an e-mail confirming. I don't want to waste your time or mine. They are equally valuable.

"I will leave the ball in your court. After I send the e-mail, if anything comes up or you change your mind for whatever reason, all I ask is you contact me to cancel. Is that fair?

"But, if I don't hear from you after I send the e-mail, I will assume no news is good news. You will see my smiling face. How does that sound?"

8. Send Outlook Invite

Be complete with your invite. In the subject, restate your name, your company, their name, their company. In the address, make it complete with street, suite, city, state, zip and even their contact phone number. In the notes section, insert your signature.

Note: We will talk more about this in later chapters. You will still send an agenda two days prior, but that is in addition.

So what did we learn about prospecting?

1. **Prepare**
2. **Ways to prospect**
3. **There are no gatekeepers**
4. **State initial benefit**
5. **Empower who you are speaking to**
6. **Ask for appointment**
7. **Confirm verbally**
8. **Send Outlook Invite**

Treat every person like they can sign on the dotted line. For all you know, they can.

CHAPTER 5

Obtain Referrals

Referrals: An effective way to earn business in which one individual endorses the services of another individual to a third party in an effort to increase everyone's income.

The 1/3, 1/3, 1/3 rule of sales as it relates to referrals:

One third of people will refer you no matter what. One third will never refer you. The middle third will decide whether to refer you based on if you ask how you ask, and what you ask.

Everybody wants to get help. Everybody wants to give help. That's what separates salespeople from consultants. When people refer you potential business, you must realize that it helps them too. If they are viewed further as a sustaining resource for their client, it helps their business, too, even if you don't pay them. True referrals never involve financial payment for the opportunity to serve others.

Have people ever answered when you ask for referrals that they would never "do that" to another person? What does that mean? Does it mean they would never *help* their friend, client, or colleague?

Think of the last big purchase you made. Someone probably referred you to that realtor, car salesperson, or accountant. If that supplier performed well, were you angry with your friend for referring you? Of course not. You appreciated it.

In your mind, your friend's status increased because your friend became a sustaining resource for you. That's referrals.

Never ask yourself why someone should give you referrals. Always ask, "Why would they not?"

The steps to obtaining referrals are:

1. **Who do you ask?**

2. **What do you ask?**

3. **Qualify/Ask for introduction**

4. **Utilize referral**

5. **Follow up with referral source**

1. Who do you ask?

People refer people they like—and people like them.

Referrals do not only come from existing customers after the service or product is delivered without any errors. If referrals could only be garnered that way, none of us would achieve success. To best obtain referrals, identify available resources. Even if someone or a company is not a candidate for your service, they may be able to refer you to someone who is.

Not everyone you meet may be a potential client, but everyone is a potential referral source to increase your revenues.

The following page is a list of suggested referral sources. (No surprise, it includes many of the same prospecting sources.)

WHO CAN REFER ME?

- Customers
- Prospects
- Friends/relatives
- Internal employees
- Vendors
- Office equipment vendor
- Office supplies vendor
- Your accountant/Your attorney/Your insurance agent
- Your local, long distance, cellular phone, hosting, Internet provider
- Your health club
- Your landlord/condo association
- Your barber/ Your grocery store manager/Your dry cleaner
- Members of associations in which you or your company have memberships
- Members of chambers of commerce in which you or your company have memberships
- Members of chambers of commerce in area in which you live or your company is located (even without membership)
- High school and college alumni organizations
- Previous employers
- Past internal employees from previous employers
- Previous prospective employers
- Competitors
- Salespeople who sell to the same clients in the same territory, but with a different product
- Salespeople who sell a complementary product in the same industry (e.g., phone equipment vendors referring phone service providers)
- Lead groups

2. What do you ask?

Now that you know who to ask, what do you say? Getting good referrals takes work. It goes beyond saying, "If you know someone who wants my services, let me know." There are steps to be conducted.

- *Personalize.*

Referrals are not about your company. They are about you. No one refers a company. They refer individuals. If referrers likes your company and your product- as of course they do or they wouldn't have bought it, that's terrific. But when it comes to referring business, you want them to focus on referring *you personally.*

- *Ask for "help."*

It's worth reiterating, the word "help" is the most powerful word in the language of business. Use this exact word.

- *Reiterate your ideal client.*

If you make it easy for people to refer you, they will. Make it hard, and they won't.

Don't just say, "Who do you know?" You are the one asking. Trigger their emotions. Get them thinking about who they know.

For instance, when TBN Sales Solutions asks for referrals, we return to the top characteristics of our ideal client.

Let's take a closer look on the following pages at how to approach the various referral scenarios and offer some suggested wording.

☐ Customer—upon the actual signing of the agreement

Reconsider the philosophy that the only time to ask for referrals is when a product or service is delivered flawlessly. What if, by chance, your company's delivery is not perfect? You are still entitled to additional clients. Mistakes happen. If salespeople limit themselves to times of errorless perfection, they miss out on tremendous opportunities.

> *The best time to ask for referrals is not after delivery, but when the agreement is signed. People are most excited when they decide to purchase your service. Anticipation produces more happiness than the event itself. Take advantage.*

Your customers do not have any doubts about what they just agreed to purchase. If they did, they wouldn't have bought. Here's a suggested script:

"So-and-So, thanks for the business. I'm excited to service your account. Can I now get your help? You know how hard jobs are like mine. Who can you refer me to? My ideal client is…Who do you know that may fit some of those parameters?"

- ☐ Customer—upon successful delivery

Yes, when a service is delivered flawlessly, take advantage that day at that moment and ask for referrals. Here's a suggested script:

"So-and-So, thanks for the business. As you see, we fulfilled our promise Can I now get your help? You know how hard jobs are like mine. Who can you refer me to? My ideal client is… Who do you know that may fit some of those parameters?"

- ☐ Customer—resolution of problems

Client don't demand that everything go perfectly after the purchase your services. Ideally, it does. But what's more important is that if there are hiccups, they are addressed and resolved. They appreciate it more than you ever know. Here's a suggested script:

OBTAIN REFERRALS

"So-and-So, I know things did not go exactly as planned. However, hopefully, you saw our ability to resolve the situation. Just as I helped you, perhaps you can now help me. You know how hard jobs are like mine. Who can you refer me to? My ideal client is… Who do you know that may fit some of those parameters?"

- Your personal/company vendors (Whoever you purchase services from)

Anybody you pay for services or products should—without hesitation—be willing to consider paying for your services. Their company may not be a candidate for your services outright. Maybe they're too small or not your target market. But referrals are always an option.

The challenge is that vendors are not in the mindset of perceiving you as the seller and them as the buyer, so you have to ask. Now they may say no and even be short. If they are short with you, frankly, I'd reconsider your business relationship.

I know with all my clients, they are at the top of my list whenever others need services they potential offer. Here's a suggested script:

"So-and-So, I need your help. You know how hard jobs are like ours. Since I have been your client during this time, I was wondering if you might be interested in our services and enable me to return the business. Who can you refer me to? My ideal client is…Who do you know that may fit some of those parameters? It would really help me."

- Prospects –even if they don't buy your services

Salespeople will sometimes click on a personal level with prospects but still not earn their business. These prospects will tell you how good you are, how much they like you, and how their decision to not purchase your services is nothing personal. If that happens, this is a great opportunity to ask for referrals. Here's a suggested script:

"So-and-So, I know we are not in a position to help you and your company at this time. But perhaps you could help me another way. I'd greatly appreciate it. You know how hard jobs are like mine. Who can you refer me to? My ideal client is…Who do you know that may fit some of those parameters? It would really help me."

- Internal employees

This includes all non-salespeople such as administrators, customer service and support. These people have many connections and already believe strongly in your company and your product. (They work with you!) Helping you bring in business makes them look good. It does not matter that they don't get commissions. Often, generating revenues for the company and for someone on their team is incentive enough. Take them to lunch. Buy them gifts. Appreciate them. Here's a suggested script:

"So-and-So, I was wondering if you could help me. You know firsthand how good our company is and the service we offer. You know how great our customer service is because that's you. Who can you refer me to? My ideal client is…Who do you know that may fit some of those parameters? It would really help me."

- Friends/relatives.

Take advantage of friends and family. They want to see you succeed more than anybody. But you do have to ask for help- specifically. Here's a suggested script:

"So-and-So, I was wondering if you could help me. I know we are in different business worlds, but you know how hard jobs

are like mine. Who do you know who may be able to benefit from our service? It would really help me."

3. Qualify/Ask for introduction

Don't stop at getting the referral. Now ask the referrer to go the extra mile. Get greedy. Don't accept only a name and a company name. Ask referrers to send an e-mail to alert the person you will call. It's terrific if they want to make a phone call, but push for that e-mail where they then cc you on the e-mail.

Do not let the referrer tell you that the other person will call you. It's critical that you be able to contact that person. If we all waited around for people to call us, none of us would have jobs. Ask for a name, the company name, phone number, and an e-mail address.

Next, you don't want to bombard the person referring you with questions, but, "If you shoot for the stars and settle for the moon, that's okay, too." Ask your new best friend questions to qualify the referral. You might ask:

- Why do you think they'd be interested?
- How big is the company?
- Have they ever had sales training? (in my case naturally)
- What would it take for the decision maker to be interested in my services?
- What motivates them?

Your referrer may not know the answers, but if they do, what great information!

Here's how it may sound after you ask for the referral:

Referrer: "Why don't you call Company XYZ? Mention my name."

Salesperson: "That's terrific. I really appreciate it. But now I am going to get greedy. Could you send them an e-mail on my behalf and then cc me. It would really help to have that introduction. You know the power of a name. I appreciate it."

Referrer: "No problem."

Salesperson: "One more thing, what do you know about their business? What's So-and-So like...?"

3. Utilize the referral

How should you utilize the referral? That's easy. Let the person referring you decide, but of course with some prompting from you.

Here's what you say:

"So-and-So, thanks for the referral. Here's what I will do with your permission. First, I will call them. I'm sure I will get voice mail. I will mention your name right on the voice mail and what I do. Then, I will follow up with an e-mail. I will say your name right in the subject line and the e-mail and cc you. But I will only do this if that's okay. Is that okay with you?"

The referrer will respect you more than you can imagine. When was the last time you referred someone business and got that e-mail as the referrer? Probably never.

Let me further emphasize this point, as the business has changed in the last ten years. You MUST get permission from the person referring you on all fronts. Do not assume that just because they gave you names, it's okay to drop their name.

Early in my sales training career, I had an experience where I did burn a bridge unnecessarily specifically by not implementing this strategy. Allow me to explain.

OBTAIN REFERRALS

One of my best clients was a realtor whose sales I tremendously increased by teaching many strategies in this book. As a result, Steve (not his real name) referred me to the owner of the firm. This resulted in at least five additional new clients who purchased books, my home study cd series and personal sales coaching. All in all, this referral system resulted in $10,000 in additional revenues for my business. The referrals didn't stop there.

The owner then referred me to even more realtors in his company.

Here's where I dropped the ball. When the owner told me to contact all the realtors, which numbered another 100, I didn't clarify the referral. I did not ask permission- as noted above- to utilize his name as a source.

When I reached out to those other realtors (via e-mail) and said his name, he was unaware of what I would be doing. I actually did blind carbon copy him on the e-mail, but a naturally busy man, apparently he was unaware or never saw the e-mails. I thought I was being very respectful by bccing him, but the problem is we hadn't talked about it prior to my activities.

One of those realtors felt pressure to purchase my services because she thought her owner was basically telling her to. When she asked the owner about it, the owner forgot that he even had referred me to his team. Not only was he furious at me, he was upset at the original realtor who first hired me and introduced me to the company himself. As a result, both my relationship with the original realtor, the owner and everywhere in between was never the same.

Had I simply asked permission and double-checked the offer, all of this would have been avoidable.

> *While referrals are about helping others, never forget people referring you are putting their name on their line to help others- and you. Triple check they want to help.*

Once you do get authorization to utilize the referral, take advantage. Have you ever referred somebody and they have not followed up? Pretty annoying, isn't it?

Too often salespeople receive referrals but fail to maximize the referrals' potential. They receive names and numbers of companies to call, but then when they contact the potential customer, they fail to mention how they received the referral's name. Why? "I didn't want to make the person who referred me mad at me for mentioning his name," the salesperson explains.

Here we go again. Mad at you? So long as you double-check- as noted above referrers voluntarily provided you a company's name and information. They did so because they wanted to help you. They felt you deserved it and were willing to wield their own influence to see you succeed. They also thought you legitimately could help someone they respect. They wanted to share that with their colleagues. If they didn't want to, they would have simply refused all your requests.

> *What does it say if someone else feels you and your service can help others, but you don't think you and your service can help others?*

Another reason salespeople do not maximize utilization of referrals is that they do not recognize the value of saying someone referred them. That is incorrect.

Saying someone else's name to someone who that other person knows but you don't is very powerful. Your new contacts may not know very well, but they do know and like your referrer. Often, that's incentive enough to hear you out.

In addition, you would be surprised, but the person you are calling based on the referrer often is flattered someone was thinking of them. Remember, people who refer you don't view it as "sicking you" on another prospect. They view it as matching two professionals they respect very much.

Since I told you a negative story that didn't work out, let me share the flip side of when it does work.

During my phone service days, I sold to individual distributors of a network marketing company that operated in a similar fashion to Amway. The company produced a special vitamin drink to boost energy. The first customers I signed up were Joe and

Carol. They came to me because my sister-in-law worked with them. Over the next six months, I signed up ten more of these network marketers in Joe and Carol's chain. Each time the business came from Joe and Carol's referrals. Each time, I used their name. Each time, the sale took five minutes. The response was always the same. "If Joe and Carol referred you, you must be good. Sign me up."

When utilizing referrals, there are some important rules to follow:

- To ensure you don't have the realtor story situation I spoke about, don't only get verbal permission, send a special e-mail to the person who referred you entitled, "Thanks for the referrals."

Here's what you say in an e-mail:

Subject: Thanks for the referrals

"So-and-So,

A quick note to say thanks for the referrals. Per our discussion, I will follow up with...."

(List their exact names, titles – and even phone numbers and e-mails – if you have it)

Any additional support you can provide would be terrific. I will keep you posted."

Sincerely,
Todd B. Natenberg

Author of, *"I've been in sales for 10 years! Now what?" A (NEW) Playbook for Skyrocketing Your Commissions*

Endorsed by Brian Tracy, Roger Dawson and Stephan Schiffman

President, TBN Sales Solutions

Phone: (816) 876-9184
e-mail: todd@toddnatenberg.com http://www.toddnatenberg.com

TBN Sales Solutions increases commissions for salespeople through customized training. We establish step-by-step sales processes with private workshops, individual consulting and keynote speaking for associations to impact the bottom line.

"Customers do not care how much you know until they know how much you care. But showing how much you care includes showing how much you care about yourself. Sell how you want to buy."

What's great about this is that you are confirming the verbal confirmation you received as noted above, you are keeping yourself organized, and you are ensuring you have the right information.

☐ In contacting the referral, lead with the name of the person who referred you.

Don't just mention their name. Say it first. The person who referred you is your in. The name could singlehandedly ensure the contact will listen to your initial benefit statement. Also, indicate how you know them. If they're a client, say so. If they're a prospect, say the prospect is considering your services or that you are "working with them." If you network together, say that. Relationships are important.

- Phone first.

As important as e-mail may be, the phone is more personal. The sound of one's voice and hearing another's name stimulates the mind more than e-mail, especially at the beginning of a business relationship. But remember when you call, the person you are calling still may not be the individual you seek. Continue to follow the previous outlined steps of how to prospect and state your initial benefit.

Here's a suggested script:

Salesperson: "Hello. Who am I speaking with?"

Secretary: "Susie."

Salesperson: Hello, Susie. My name is Todd Natenberg, and I'm the president of TBN Sales Solutions. John Smith from company XYZ referred me to Steve Jones. Is Steve in?"

Secretary: "No, he's not. Can I take a message? What's this regarding?"

Salesperson: "The reason I'm calling is TBN Sales Solutions…"

Often, the conversation the salesperson has with secretaries and receptionists when utilizing referrals is just as critical as the conversation they will have with the person they actually want to meet. If the salesperson upsets the message receiver, your contact could care less who you know.

- Leave voice mail on the direct line.

We spoke earlier about always leaving voice mail messages when prospecting. With a referral, request voice mail if the person you are contacting is unavailable. You can leave a message with the secretary too, but for the referral to have its utmost power, it's important the person you are contacting knows you are not cold-calling.

Often, the secretary will not relay this vital information. You want that person to actually hear your voice and the name of the friend who referred you. You want them to know who told you to call, why they told you to call, and why they should care that their friend told you to call.

Here's a sample script for the voice mail message:

"Hello, So-and-So. This is Todd Natenberg, President, TBN Sales Solutions, (816) 876-9184- So-and-So from Such-and-Such referred me. They thought I could help your company. My organization increases commissions for salespeople…"

- E-mail if you can't reach them.

Don't think just because contacts don't call you back, they aren't interested. People are busy. You told your referral source what you would do. Now do it. You need to create a sense of urgency. Creating a sense of urgency comes in part from making your message clear, concise, and available by all means possible. E-mail is one of these means.

Here are some additional e-mail rules to adhere to:

- ☐ If the referral does not call back within one day, send e-mail referencing your unsuccessful phone attempts.

- ☐ The e-mail must begin with the name of the person who referred you.

- ☐ Say in email exactly why you are sending information.

- ☐ Enclose information or link further demonstrating your benefits.

- ☐ Again, cc your referral (After all you told them you would).

Case in point, I will never forget one occasion where I referred my own mortgage broker to another individual to earn their business. I never did find out what happened- until six months later when I bumped into that individual who I referred my mortgage broker to. As it turns out, that person had bought a mortgage from my mortgage broker.

Not only did I never know they connected, I never received even close to a "thank you" from the mortgage broker. Frankly, not only did I never refer the broker again, I told every person I met to not use him.

> *People are 10 times more likely to complain about bad service that compliments good service. Make sure you are on the right side of the equation.*

If people refer you, practice common courtesy by keeping them informed about the status of the opportunity. By keeping them up-to-date, they also can continue to help you land the new client. How powerful that would be if the next time Susie and my client spoke, my client asked Susie about the status of Bob's deal.

"Oh, you know about that?" Susie might ask.

"Of course," my client replies. "I referred you to Bob. How's he doing?"

"Fine. I guess. I'm just not sure…I'm glad you brought it up. I actually have a couple questions for you…"

> *The more people who know what you are doing, the more people you have to help you do what you are doing.*

SAMPLE REFERRAL E-MAIL.

Subject: So-and-So referred me—Skyrocketing sales for XXX

CC: So-and-So

Prospect So-and-So (always use their first name),
So-and-So recommended I contact you.

I'm Todd Natenberg, and I am the president of TBN Sales Solutions, as well as the author of the book *"I've been in sales for 10 years! Now what?"*

TBN Sales Solutions increases commissions for salespeople through customized training. We establish step-by-step sales processes through private workshops, individual consulting and keynote speaking for associations to impact the bottom line.

Per my voice mail, I'm looking forward to helping your business.

John, who is a customer of mine (or who I know through mutual networking contacts, the chamber of commerce, LinkedIn, etc.), had good things to say about you and your business. He thought perhaps we could help.

I have enclosed materials for your convenience. I also encourage you to visit www.toddnatenberg.com for more information.

After you have had a chance to review the materials, I would like to schedule an in-person appointment to review your needs.

Please call me at (816) 876-9184 or e-mail with questions. I look forward to speaking with you soon.

PS: So-and-So, thanks for the terrific referral. I will keep you posted.

Sincerely,
Todd B. Natenberg

Author of, *"I've been in sales for 10 years! Now what?" A (NEW) Playbook for Skyrocketing Your Commissions*

Endorsed by Brian Tracy, Roger Dawson and Stephan Schiffman

President, TBN Sales Solutions

Phone: (816) 876-9184
e-mail: todd@toddnatenberg.com
http://www.toddnatenberg.com
www.ijustgotajobinsales.com

TBN Sales Solutions increases commissions for salespeople through customized training. We establish step-by-step sales processes with private workshops, individual consulting and keynote speaking for associations to impact the bottom line.

"Customers do not care how much you know until they know how much you care. But showing how much you care includes showing how much you care about yourself. Sell how you want to buy."

After the e-mail is sent, call one more time. If you get voice mail once again, leave another message complete with your initial benefit. If you still don't get a response back, move on and put the prospect in your tickler file.

5. Follow up with referral source

While we talked about carbon copying your referrer, there is one more step after that initial e-mail. This is the follow-up. From here on, you don't use the cc feature. However, any time you correspond with your new prospect, forward that e-mail to whoever referred you. It's a way to say thank you. They will appreciate it.

Lastly, if the referral becomes a true client, you need to go thank-you crazy. First, call up the referrer via phone and leave a voice mail thanking them.

Finally, take a moment and write a personal thank-you note. Send it via snail mail. It's the least you can do. They will appreciate it.

So what did we learn about referrals?

1. **Who do you ask?**

2. **What do you ask?**

3. **Qualify**

4. **Utilize referral**

5. **Follow up with referral source**

> *Referrals are much more than a name and a number. They are qualified opportunities that are mutually beneficial to not only the salesperson, but the person doing the referring as well.*

CHAPTER 6:

Build the Business Case

> Sales call: An appointment with a firm date and time with the goal of uncovering prospects' needs, desires, and hot buttons to provide solutions that result in the advancement of the sale.

Customers do not care how much you know until they know how much you care...but showing how much you care goes way beyond asking the right questions.

You have organized yourself. You have earned the right to sell. You have created interest by stating your initial benefit articulately. You have solidified the appointment with a firm date and time. All of these steps have been the buildup to this moment: running the sales appointment.

Through your previous strategies, you have positioned yourself as not just another salesperson. You've made it clear you are a consultant. To continue the process effectively, you must now execute that which you have promised you will.

> *The one who asks the most questions wins. What do people like to talk about most? Themselves. Give prospects what they want.*

Learn about prospects. Ask questions to uncover needs. Build your business case. If all goes as planned, the business case will demonstrate why the prospect would be crazy not to purchase your product.

In this chapter, we will present the playbook for building a business case, otherwise known as running a sales call:

1. **Confirm appointment (but not how you think)**
2. **Wait like a pro**
3. **Set the agenda**
4. **Probe**
5. **Summarize**
6. **Present**
7. **Close**

1. Confirm appointment (but not how you think)

In old-school sales, they taught you to never confirm the appointment. They said you risked prospects changing their mind. Good! Let them. Change their mind from what? You helping them? You are a consultant. Consultants don't get points for running meetings. They get points for earning new clients.

If prospects are going to cancel meetings based on what you will be taught in a moment to do, they certainly had no interest in buying from you in the first place.

In my personal 20 years of selling, managing, and training, I have found that there is no better strategy that has worked more effectively than what I call the PAL—purpose, agenda, limit.

The PAL is not the ordinary agenda that many salespeople claim they send. I can't emphasize that enough: What they CLAIM they send. If you are someone who sends an agenda, you are in the top 1 percent. Reps do not do that, no matter what they say.

So, what is the PAL? The PAL is a confirmation, an outline, an affirmation of logistics, and a preview of what everyone will discuss at a meeting. It's a very powerful tool.

When I worked for LCI International in suburban Chicago, I once scheduled a meeting with the owner of a lumber company. I sent the PAL prior to the meeting. When I arrived, the prospect said, "I don't remember who you are, but I got your fax (no e-mail back then). Obviously, we spoke, and I just forgot. But I was so impressed with this form that I now have to consider switching to LCI. And I want you to know I am having each of my sales reps send these to their prospects."

Before we dissect each part of the PAL, the following pages are templates for the most common sales appointments:

FIRST APPOINTMENT SAMPLE PAL E-MAIL

Subject: Agenda for in-person meeting on Thursday at 1:30 p.m. with TBN Sales Solutions

So-and-So,

Per our conversation, this is to confirm our appointment tomorrow, Thursday, Nov. 11, at 1:30 p.m. at your office:

3295 XYZ Rd., Ste. 1, Chicago, IL 60061, (555) 555-5555.

If anything has changed, please call me at (816) 876-9184. However, if I don't hear from you, I will assume we are on as scheduled.

In the meantime, I encourage you to visit us at www.ijustgotajobin-sales.com for more information if you have not already.

Purpose:

To review your company's sales training needs to consider a potential investment in TBN Sales Solutions.

Agenda:

- Learn more about your company's goals.
- Examine your sales training needs.
- Review TBN Sales Solutions programs relating to these goals and needs.
- Sign necessary paperwork to hire TBN Sales Solutions.

Limit:

½ hour

Attending:

So-and-So, (555) 555-5555
Todd Natenberg, President, TBN Sales Solutions (816) 876-9184

Sincerely,
Todd B. Natenberg

Author of, *"I've been in sales for 10 years! Now what?" A (NEW) Playbook for Skyrocketing Your Commissions*

Endorsed by Brian Tracy, Roger Dawson and Stephan Schiffman

President, TBN Sales Solutions

Phone: (816) 876-9184
e-mail: todd@toddnatenberg.com
http://www.toddnatenberg.com
www.ijustgotajobinsales.com

TBN Sales Solutions increases commissions for salespeople through customized training. We establish step-by-step sales processes with private workshops, individual consulting and keynote speaking for associations to impact the bottom line.

"Customers do not care how much you know until they know how much you care. But showing how much you care includes showing how much you care about yourself. Sell how you want to buy."

Let's examine each section.

- *Subject: Agenda for...*

We live in a fast-paced world now, a world filled with spam- and virus-filled information. Nobody has time for anything. Prospects—even hot ones who meet with you—will only read e-mail if they see the value immediately. Make that e-mail one point and one point only. Not only that, where are 95% of e-mails read today? On the phone, so you have to be even more direct than ever.

Also, by saying agenda, it will make it easy for you to organize yourself, which I've stated previously is another amazing benefit of sending e-mail. Your "agenda" e-mails will be your hot prospects when you go look for them down the road in your sent file.

> **The easier salespeople make it for their prospects to be organized and attentive to their services, the more attentive they will be.**

- *Per our conversation, this is to confirm our appointment tomorrow, Wednesday, Nov. 11, at 1:30 p.m. at your office:*

3295 XYZ Rd., Ste. 1, Chicago, IL 60061 (555) 555-5555

If anything has changed, please call me at (816) 876-9184.

Like we said earlier, when something appears in writing, it is real. It is the same for your prospects. When you show how serious you are, they will take you just as seriously. By further confirming your phone conversation when you scheduled the appointment, you leave the ball in their court.

But in reality, you are in control. If you do not hear from them, you will meet. You said it when you spoke. You confirmed it via e-mail.

If they want to cancel now, let them. They either honestly had something come up or had no interest. Either way, you are valuing both your time and that of the prospect.

These sentences also provide important logistics. They tell where you are meeting, the time of the meeting, and how to reach one another. When driving to the meeting, you will now have all the information readily available. If for any reason the location has changed or you misunderstood information, it easily can be clarified. Everyone is held accountable.

In addition, notice even the spacing in the e-mail. Break out the address to completely verify you are both on the same page. More than once, I've had prospects correct my misunderstanding for locations. Everybody wins this way.

- *Purpose:*

To review your company's sales training needs to consider a potential investment in TBN Sales Solutions

Unless expressly spelled out, your agenda may not be the prospect's agenda. The "purpose" establishes you as a professional who has a specific plan, ensures that your purpose is the same as the prospect's, and eliminates surprises for both of you.

- *Agenda:*

    - Learn more about XXX
    - Examine sales training goals and needs
    - Review TBN Sales Solutions' programs relating to these goals and needs
    - Sign necessary paperwork to hire TBN Sales Solutions

Let's address the sign necessary paperwork" comment for a moment.
This will depend on where you feel you are in the sales process. If this is too much for you, don't do it. If you're selling a large-ticket

item (i.e., when I sold government accounts with Discovery), it may not be appropriate.

But if your item is transactional, go for it. If this is your ideal client, take the chance. You will not upset the prospect. Here's a shocker: They know you are a salesperson trying to earn their business! They expect it, and respect it.

Other suggested wording could be phrases such as, "verbal commitment to recommend TBN Sales Solutions" or "schedule training dates."

If prospects think you are too aggressive, they will either tell you via e-mail or otherwise indicate that your sale may not be as far along as you want it to be. Either way, that last sentence has to be whatever your "maximum goal" is for the appointment.

If they are taken aback and send their thoughts via e-mail, don't panic. Simply respond with "No problem. I appreciate you being up-front, but let's still meet. Frankly, that's why I sent the agenda. I wanted to be sure we are on the same page. Now I know where we stand. See you Thursday."

> *The goal of running a sales appointment is either to close the deal or advance the sales process to a firm follow-up date and time. Nothing less.*

- *Limit: ½ hour*

Tell the prospect how much time to budget. A half hour is recommended. Some sales managers and trainers will ask for fifteen or twenty minutes, but be careful about estimating low. When was the last time you ran a true sales call in a short twenty minutes?

Be realistic. If you put a time limit, stick to it. Don't ask for twenty minutes if you know you need an hour. (We will address this more in a moment when we actually get to what to say on the sales appointment itself).

- *Attending:*

    So-and-So, (555) 555-5555

Todd Natenberg, President, (816) 876-9184

Have you ever been on a sales call where you brought along your sales manager, the sales engineer, and the customer service person, and someone had to stand because there was not enough space? That situation would be easily avoided had you let the prospect know beforehand who would attend.

Also, if you alert prospects that you are bringing your manager or specialist, they can decide whether they want to invite others from their company. Bringing managers impresses prospects because it shows you value their business. Team selling rocks.

In addition, whenever possible- if the prospects had indicated prior that others would attend the appointment, remind them of those individuals to invite.

The following pages include other sample PALS.

SECOND APPOINTMENT (PROPOSAL) SAMPLE PAL E-MAIL

Subject: Agenda for in-person meeting on Thursday at 1:30 p.m. with TBN Sales Solutions

So-and-So,

Per our conversation, this is to confirm our appointment tomorrow, Thursday, Nov. 11, at 1:30 p.m. at your office:

3295 XYZ Rd., Ste. 1, Chicago, IL 60061, (555) 555-5555.

If anything has changed, please call me at (816) 876-9184. However, if I don't hear from you, I will assume we are on as scheduled.

Purpose:

To present a solution to increase your sales revenues through a strategic investment in TBN Sales Solutions.

Agenda:

- Update on your sales training goals and needs

(Note: list what their goals and needs are based on previous conversations and appointment)

- Present TBN Sales Solutions programs relating to these goals and needs.

(Note: list here your recommendations in succinct bullet point form, or a link to your website, or even an attachment outlining your ideas)

- Sign necessary paperwork to hire TBN Sales Solutions.

Limit:

½ hour

Attending:

So-and-So, (555) 555-5555
Todd Natenberg, President, TBN Sales Solutions (816) 876-9184

Sincerely,
Todd B. Natenberg

Author of, *"I've been in sales for 10 years! Now what?" A (NEW) Playbook for Skyrocketing Your Commissions*

Endorsed by Brian Tracy, Roger Dawson and Stephan Schiffman

President, TBN Sales Solutions

Phone: (816) 876-9184
e-mail: todd@toddnatenberg.com
http://www.toddnatenberg.com
www.ijustgotajobinsales.com

TBN Sales Solutions increases commissions for salespeople through customized training. We establish step-by-step sales processes with private workshops, individual consulting and keynote speaking for associations to impact the bottom line.

"Customers do not care how much you know until they know how much you care. But showing how much you care includes showing how much you care about yourself. Sell how you want to buy."

NETWORKING APPOINTMENT- SAMPLE PAL E-MAIL

Subject: Agenda for in-person meeting on Thursday at 1:30 p.m. with TBN Sales Solutions

So-and-So,

Per our conversation, this is to confirm our appointment tomorrow, Thursday, Nov. 11, at 1:30 p.m. at your office:

3295 XYZ Rd., Ste. 1, Chicago, IL 60061, (555) 555-5555.

If anything has changed, please call me at (816) 876-9184. However, if I don't hear from you, I will assume we are on as scheduled.

Purpose:

To discuss mutual networking opportunities to increase both our revenues through a strategic partnership

Agenda:

- Who is So-and-So? What does the company of So-and-So do?
- Who is Todd Natenberg? What does TBN Sales Solutions do?
- Discuss mutual networking opportunities

Limit:

½ hour

Attending:

So-and-So, (555) 555-5555
Todd Natenberg, President, TBN Sales Solutions (816) 876-9184

Sincerely,
Todd B. Natenberg

Author of, *"I've been in sales for 10 years! Now what?" A (NEW) Playbook for Skyrocketing Your Commissions*

Endorsed by Brian Tracy, Roger Dawson and Stephan Schiffman

President, TBN Sales Solutions

Phone: (816) 876-9184
e-mail: todd@toddnatenberg.com
http://www.toddnatenberg.com
www.ijustgotajobinsales.com

TBN Sales Solutions increases commissions for salespeople through customized training. We establish step-by-step sales processes with private workshops, individual consulting and keynote speaking for associations to impact the bottom line.

"Customers do not care how much you know until they know how much you care. But showing how much you care includes showing how much you care about yourself. Sell how you want to buy."

Using the PAL does not mean appointments will never cancel. They will, but almost always they will cancel prior to the meeting. The prospect will send an e-mail or call to inform you of a change in plans. That's okay. Better to get the cancellation prior to the meeting than to go out and meet with someone who's not really interested. Utilizing this strategy and the days of prospects "blowing you off" are long gone.

On the rare occasion that you do go to meet with a prospect and the prospect is nowhere to be found, a printout of your PAL becomes your greatest tool. Here's how it works if that rare time occurs when you arrive for an appointment and the prospect is nowhere to be found.

Salesperson (showing your PAL to the secretary):

"I'm so sorry. I even confirmed the appointment. Here's a printout of the e-mail I sent. I hope everything's okay. I certainly was not trying to intrude, but when I did not hear from So-and-So, I thought we were on. See?"

Secretary: "No, I'm the one who's sorry. That's unlike him. Let me get him on his cell phone. That's not right."

In most cases, prospects feel so guilty about your professionalism and their lack of professionalism that they want to reschedule a solid appointment. "It's my fault," they say, graciously apologizing more often than not. "I know I should have called. Can we reschedule it? What works for you?"

Just a reminder, if your meeting came from a referral, two other things:

Forward the agenda to whoever referred you. Don't cc them on the e-mail. That is overkill. Remember, at this point the prospect agreed to meet with you. Your referrer got you in the door, but you are on your own now.

Still, like we said, keep your referrer in the loop. Yes, you have your own relationships with that person, but your referrer's is still better. They see your prospect more than you see them. It's another bullet in your arsenal.

2. Wait like a pro (There still are no gatekeepers)

When does a sales appointment start? The minute you walk through the door. More than once, I've seen a terrific salesperson destroy a meeting by being unprofessional with the person up front. The same rules apply in prospecting: because you never know with whom you are speaking.

The first person who sees you may as well be the person with whom you are meeting. For all you know, that person will also attend the meeting.

When I was a sales manager interviewing candidates for jobs, the first person I approached after the interview was our secretary to see what she thought of the candidate based on her interaction. I knew that how a candidate would act in front of me should be no different than how that candidate would act when I was not watching.

> *When people make the absurd comments that they can't get into sales because they can't lie, cheat, or be pushy, I explain to them, "You know what those salespeople are called who do that? UNEMPLOYED.*

If you've been here before and you know the receptionist, be just as friendly as you were the last time. Greet the receptionist by name, shake hands, provide a business card, and tell them with whom you have an appointment and at what time. Hopefully, you've treated them with such respect, you remember their name.

This last part is critical. Some front desk people question salespeople unnecessarily. If the person you are scheduled to meet is on the phone, the receptionist may refuse to interrupt. This can pose a problem because time can pass while the prospect remains on the phone. It's a never-ending circle.

Prospects often only stay on the phone because they don't realize you are waiting outside. The longer you wait, the more upset they grow, because they think you are late. If this appears to be happening, politely, but sternly, say to the person upfront

"If you could just please tell So-and-So I'm here, I'd appreciate it. We are slated to meet at XXX. I've had it happen more than once that customers remain on the phone or in a meeting because they think I'm not here. I appreciate the help."

It's bold, but necessary. Stand your ground.

As part of the waiting, don't forget to do the necessary research. Notice your surroundings. Read the awards on the wall. Glance through the magazines. Probing for hot buttons already has begun. (You also will do all this in the meeting when you first get back there).

3. Set the Agenda

At last, you and your prospect are meeting face-to-face. How you act in the next twenty seconds will determine how long this meeting lasts and whether your prospect will be interested. Take nothing for granted:

- Say hello with a firm handshake and a smile.
- Give the prospect a business card.

Yes, have some chitchat:

"How have you been?"
"How's the weather?"
"Did you see the Chicago Cubs/Kansas City Royals game?"

But time yourself. Keep this to just a couple minutes. It's important you set that agenda right away. Then you can get into the banter.

As you are explaining the agenda, hand the prospect a printout of the PAL. Reference the document in your discussion.

Here's how it works:

"Thanks, So-and-So, for meeting with me. I'm glad our schedules could match up. I don't want to waste your time or mine. They are equally valuable.

"What I would like to do- as indicated here in the e-mail I sent you- is learn more about your company, including what you are looking for in the areas of sales training, if anything. Then, I'd like to tell you a little bit about TBN Sales Solutions as it relates to your needs. If there's a potential fit, we'll go from there.

"This meeting should take no more than a half an hour. If it goes longer, though, because you are asking good questions and there's an interest, then you can't kick me out. How does that sound?"

This immediately puts you on the same professional level as the prospect. Telling them up front that their time is no more valuable than yours may sound direct, but trust me when I say it's an incredible strategy that works. Say it politely, but with confidence. Prospects will appreciate you taking your own job seriously.

Next, note the length of the meeting. Just because you sent an e-mail saying the meeting will take a half hour, don't expect prospects to remember. Things may have come up. Perhaps prospects do not have a half hour now. Perhaps they have more. The best way to find out is to ask.

Don't be afraid to cancel a meeting if you suspect it will not go according to plan, even after you are seated in front of your prospect. Remember it's about a quality meeting, not a quantity meeting.

If a prospect appears worried or distracted, ask the prospect what's wrong. Perhaps something occurred prior to your arrival that has diverted the prospect's attention from your meeting. If this is the case, offer to reschedule. It's a tough thing to do, but your prospect will appreciate it in the long run. Better to waste your drive time than to sacrifice two hours of opportunity time.

Here's how it would sound- if need be:

"Is everything okay, So-and-So? It seems like your heart is not in this and that your mind is on other things. I can appreciate that. I'll tell you what. The information we are reviewing is very important. I don't want us to rush through the materials. That won't help either one of us. Why don't we reschedule this for another time?"

> *Knowing when to walk away is sometimes just as important as knowing when to proceed.*

4. Probe

You've heard it before, but it's worth saying again: Probing is the most important step in the sales process. But it's not just that you probe that matters, but how you probe. This is the point that is lost on salespeople. You can't just ask questions for the sake of asking questions. You have to listen. You have to be like a prosecutor or a detective.

Think of television shows like *Law and Order*. (10 years ago, we referenced *Columbo*. See how times have changed.) The cops don't just start attacking the suspects:

"Did you do it? Did you do it? Admit it. Admit it. Admit it!" – wouldn't be too effective now, would it? Of course not. They have a system.

They start off with open-ended pleasant questions, and then get more direct, and then the hardest questions are the final ones. Probing in the sales world is no different.

Before we get into the questions to ask, it's important you understand why you probe.

Frequently clients ask how I transition from newspaper reporter to a salesperson to a sales manager to a sales trainer. Actually, journalists and salespeople have very similar personalities.

Like journalists, salespeople must have thick skins. They encourage people to talk and share their wants and desires. Salespeople, too, must be curious and appreciate the power of information. A reporter develops an "angle" for a story based on interviews, while a salesperson develops a "solution" based on questioning. Both probe.

It's no surprise when I first left journalism to sell photocopiers and fax machines, my first 10 appointments were with my best sources.

"Of course, I will consider buying a copier from you, Todd," the South Barrington, Illinois mayor, who owned a law practice told me.

"I trusted you with my integrity and reputation every day. If you can help me with office equipment, that would even be easier."

> *The best salespeople I know are the best people I know. They genuinely care about people, want to help, want to connect, want to listen and understand that no person can truly serve another without also serving themselves.*

In probing, you want to accomplish the following:

- Build alliances to tie back during the presentation

> *People like to do business with people they like and people like them.*

Think about your best friend. Why is that person your best friend? The two of you undoubtedly have things in common. You may not have identical interests, but perhaps your values are the same, your religion is the same, or you may have grown up in the same neighborhood. Similarities are a large part of why you connect. Selling is no different.

Back in my LCI phone service days, one of my first clients was a small computer company. At the time I sold the account, I was going through a divorce. Ironically, so was the prospect, although I did not know it at the time.

One afternoon, we had a sales meeting to analyze his phone bill. It was getting late and my prospect still hadn't decided whether to purchase. He told me to call him next week because he had to meet with his attorney to discuss his pending divorce.

"I know what you mean," I replied. "I'm going through a divorce right now. What a nightmare."

"You're having a nightmare?" he answered. "You want a nightmare? Let me tell you what this thing is costing me…"

Ten minutes later, we had a signed deal.

Don't worry. Divorce is not the only way to build alliances with your prospects. More conventional ways include having similar target clients, such as both of you targeting small and midsized businesses, earning customers through referrals, or sharing similar keys to success, such as providing top-notch customer service.

The key is to ascertain information to build alliances, which you ultimately will tie back later in the presentation.

- Reveal the buying criteria prospects will use

If you do not know what prospects will base their buying decisions on, how can you sell to them? What you think is important and what prospects think is important don't always coincide. Studies have proven that, contrary to popular belief, people do not buy on price in most cases. But if you ask salespeople why they lose deals, many will tell you it was because their price was too high. Often, the real reason wasn't that the price was too high, but rather that prospects didn't find the solution cost-effective. In other words, they didn't find the critical element: Value.

If everything was based on price, there would be no need for salespeople. If you sell on price, you lose on price.

Of course, there are situations where the lowest per-unit cost makes or breaks the opportunity, but it's nowhere near as often as you think. If this is one of those times, you have to let prospects say this aloud. Don't say it for them.

Think about your own buying habits. Do you always buy the least expensive product? When we say "least expensive," what are we comparing it to? If something is the cheapest but it does not meet our needs, who cares what it costs?

Recently, I bought a new car. I was looking for a black, Toyota Rav for my wife and four -year-old twin sons to enjoy. The salesperson showed me a black, four-door Rav. But the price tag included shampooing the car mats and polishing the car. These added items would cost me $500, and I didn't need them. Here's what happened:

"I'll throw it in," the salesperson offered.
"But I don't want them," I contended.
"I'll throw it in," he repeated.
"I guess if you are willing to lower the price by $500, then okay," I answered.
"No," he answered. "But I said I'd throw it in."

When I told him I was confused, he said he'd "throw them in" for the $500 cost. "But I don't want the shampooing and polishing, nor do I need it," I answered angrily.

"I'm throwing it in," he foolishly argued once again.

I tried an analogy he would understand. "Do you play golf?" I asked. "Let's say someone offers to sell me a set of golf clubs for $10. That's an amazing price for an entire set of clubs. But it's not a good deal if I have no arms or legs!"

> *There is no better way to lose a sale than to not listen to a client, lie to a client or be condescending to a client. Sell how you want to buy.*

- Understand the prospect's buying process

Yes, they hopefully have explained it during your phone call the buying process for this project. But recognize whatever was spoken on the phone, or even sent via e-mail is the past is forgotten. A sale is about focusing on the here and now. Reiterate it. Here's what you say in two parts:

"Prospect So-and-So, just to reiterate. Please walk me again through the buying process."

"And so I understand the key players, in addition to you, who else will be involved in that processes? Are you the one who signs on the dotted line?"

If they indicate at that moment, they aren't the one who signs or they aren't the decision maker, you must call them out. You don't cancel the meeting, but you say directly:

You: "**Does that (signer/decision maker) know we are meeting?**"

Prospect: "**No.**"

You: "**I'm confused. Why not?**"

This is very telling. It's okay and often important to meet with non-decision-makers, but if the true decision-maker does not know what is going on, that's a huge red flag. It may be so much so that you may want to end the meeting.

> *Better to not meet with someone, to not speak on the phone, to not do a proposal, to not send an e-mail, than to go through everything only to find out there was no chance from the start.*

But don't just start canceling meetings without thinking it through. As we stated previously, often you may still need to meet with that non decision maker. The key though now is understanding your goal is gain that person's help to get to the decision maker.

> *Different meetings have different goals, different decision makers, and different processes. All are important-depending on the situation.*

- Uncover hidden pain

In the old days, this was called "cut and gush." While I know the choice of words does not sound very professional or "consultative," the reality is this is what you are trying to accomplish. It's not about manipulation. It's about uncovering a need that was there but that the prospect may have been unaware. Former president Bill Clinton said it best: "I feel your pain."

It's very similar to the role of a journalist. For all those who criticize journalists, when it comes to the sensitive interview with say, the death of a loved one, my job was to ask the right questions to have my sources reveal their innermost thoughts. As much as the questions might seem uncomfortable, whether as a journalist or as a salesperson- they need to be asked. When the right ones are asked, professionally, sensitively and with the goal to help, everyone appreciates it.

> *Seek to understand before you seek to be understood. That's selling. That's life.*

- Uncover two hot buttons that will enable you to present a solution to meet their needs

As you will see in a moment, once you discover the pain, you then try to find what will provide them a solution. Probing will enable you to discover why they would buy your services.

So, what are the questions? Here are the best questions to ask and the order to ask them:

- **"John. I know we talked over the phone and I did look at your website and did some research on your company. Still, to better understand your business and where I can help with your specific needs, I'd like to ask some questions. Is that okay?"**

Sometimes prospect have a specific agenda and want to get into it right away. But more often they simply don't know what they don't know. It is your job to guide them. In contrast, though, there are those rare occasions when they want to call the shots. Asking this upfront question disarms them right away.

- **"Before we get into it, let me just remind you in a nutshell what we do and how we came to meet. As I indicated, So-and-So referred me to you. He's a customer of mine. He thought we could help you the way we are helping him. To refresh your memory, TBN Sales Solutions…(initial benefit statement). Does that make sense?"**

Next, pause. Let prospects digest what you say. See if they have any questions before you even ask yours. But be cautious. All you are looking for is a nod of the head. You actually don't want the prospect to bombard you with questions at this point. You want to do the bombarding. You want to gather information from the prospect, not have the prospect gather information from you.

Another reason to pause is to evaluate the prospect. Watch the prospect's reaction. It will help as you forge ahead. If the prospect jumps in with "I just want to know the price," it's very telling. Don't immediately respond, but do alter your style to focus more on business.

- **"Tell me a little bit about your business."**

It's very important when asking this question that you let prospects answer however they want. Pay close attention to the answers. Often, their answer to this one question will provide you the information you would normally need through several other questions.

- **"What has been the key to your success?"**

Why is this a great question to ask? When was the last time you were asked this as a buyer? How would this make you feel? Pretty spectacular, right?

This also tells you their own buying criteria. If people like to do business with people they like and people like them, this tells you how to be like them. Throughout much of the future conversation, you will now say, "Much you like said earlier why you are successful, well we are the same way…"

- **"What is your biggest challenge with (whatever product you are selling) (i.e. from a sales training perspective?)?"**

I think this one is self-explanatory. It uncovers hidden pain.

- **"What is your role in the buying process? Who signs on the dotted line? Is that you?"**

Even if you spoke about it on the phone, you need to ask them again to ensure you know with who you are speaking. Again, if they don't sign, it doesn't mean you don't talk to them, but you need true verbalization of who you are speaking with. Let them acknowledge it themselves.

- **"What would you rate your current vendor for (whatever product you are selling) on scale of 1-10 with 10 being the highest? Why not a ten?**
- **(Follow up: "If something happened, can you please walk me through it. What did that cost your business?"**

- **(Follow up again) "What would that do to your business if you had that situation with one of your clients and your treated them that way?**
- **For you to say the delivery of our service was successful, if you invest, what will we have accomplished two months later?**

Here are a list of other great secondary questions to ask- if time permits?

- Who is your target customer?
- How do you get clients?
- What separates your business from others in the industry?
- What are your company's goals?
- How did you come by this position?
- What brought you to this company?
- What do you like most about your job?
- Regardless of whether your purchase my services, what is your time frame when you would like to have the product delivered?
- Regardless of whether you purchase my services, what is your time frame when you would like to select the vendor complete with issuing a purchase order?
- What criteria did you use the last time you made a large purchase?
- What criteria did you use the last time you switched vendors?

Remember, the key with all of these questions is to obtain the answers with the prospect verbally airing these themselves. If prospects reveal all this information with you asking only the one question, "Tell me about your business," that's terrific. That's why it's important to listen.

But what is critical here is they say the answers out loud. In the television series *Seinfeld*, the character of George Costanza once advised Jerry on how to lie. Now, let me preface this, I am NOT saying to ever lie under any circumstances, but George's point is valid. "It's not a lie, if you believe it," he says.

If you say it or I say it, it doesn't matter. If they say it, it's true.

5. Summarize

This is an easy way to distinguish you, because few salespeople do it. Be sure you understand the answers to all your questions. Prove that you listened, not just heard.

What's the difference between listening and hearing? Hearing is simply not being deaf. But listening entails a three-step process.

At TBN Sales Solutions, we call it the ART method:

- Acknowledge
- Repeat
- Take action

Let's take this one at a time.

Acknowledge

Have you ever had a one-way conversation where you do all the talking? Isn't that just as annoying as when someone else does all the talking? You feel like you are talking to a brick wall.

Then, when you address the situation, what's the other person's response? "I heard you. What was I supposed to say? I didn't know it called for a comment." What the other person doesn't understand is that you wanted acknowledgment. You needed to understand your words didn't' fall on deaf ears.

Ways to acknowledge include nodding your head with direct eye contact, positive or negative facial expressions, and verbal comments such as "I understand" or "I know what you mean."

Repeat

Typically, when salespeople acknowledge prospects, they feel they've listened. But this is just the first step. The second step is actually repeating what was just said to ensure you interpreted it properly.

Returning to our journalism comparisons. How is it those two reporters can attend the same press conference, hear a source say the same thing, and write about it differently in each newspaper? This happens in spite of the fact that both reporters have tape recorders! It's because one hears and the other listens.

The best way to avoid this problem is to repeat exactly what you hear. Don't dissect every sentence. Just hit the high points. If you did not get every point down, that's okay. Just repeat what you remember.

In hearing you repeat it, the prospect will be so impressed that what you leave out won't matter.

Take Action

This proves you truly understand the prospect's needs. What you say or do next must be a direct response to the answers provided. Many sales reps have lost deals or won deals at this step.

Here's an example of what not to do.

During my corporate training days, a rep and I probed one prospect with good questions. We reached the point where the prospect told us, "What really matters to me is reliability and customer service. Price is not the issue. If you can guarantee me your company can provide these two criteria, you will earn my business."

The rep's response was, "Great, let me show you how we can save you money. By switching to us, we will lower your rate."

The meeting ended ten minutes later. We never heard from the prospect again.

Here's some suggested wording:

"Okay, Prospect So-and-So. Let me summarize what you said. You have been with the company for 10 years. You came here from Idaho because you found it to be a great opportunity. One of the key reasons for the company's success is customer service. Your company sells to small and midsized businesses.

You are the one who would sign on the dotted line. What is important to you now are billing, customer service, and a competitive price. Is there anything I left out in terms of what's important to you and your company? "No? Then let me tell you how we can help."

6. Present

It's finally your turn to talk. So what do you say? How will your product and company help this prospect based on all the information you just ascertained? You properly pointed out there's a problem. It's your job to prove you know how to fix it.

You don't want to sound as if you're reading a script, but a written presentation is necessary at this point. An effective presentation will answer the following:

- Who is your company?
- Why and how it has been successful?
- Who are you?
- Why and how have you been successful?
- What is the product you are offering this prospect to fix the problem?
- How will this product fix the problem?
- What does it cost?
- Sign here!

When presenting, have as many visuals as possible to answer the above questions. Remember our philosophy about seeing things is that when we see it, it becomes real. This is similar to setting goals. You are not the only one who believes something more when it is written down. Your prospect will too. Some suggestions for a top-notch presentation follow.

Presentations today are different than ten years ago. They can't be more than ten minutes at the most. If you are still a Power Point fan, that would mean five visual slides.

- One slide showing your company's history
- One slide with testimonials about you and your company
- One slide of who you are personally (your personal profile, which I will detail in a moment)
- One slide showing what you actually offer (your features)

- One slide showing how the service is delivered with a timeframe

Note: Price comes after your presentation once the prospect is on board with everything else.

That's not to say you won't say more, but visually they want to see no more. Forget the bells and whistles. If you have a website, you may want to take them to it either on their computer or your own. They will appreciate it.

That's your entire presentation. Everything else will involve how to overcome objections. You will have 50 more sales tools, but those will only be used if requested.

> ***The simpler you make the sale, the simpler it is. The simpler it is, the easier for prospects to buy. The easier for them to buy, the more they will.***

The most important part of your presentation is being able to answer questions the customer may have. They may not ask them, but if they do, you should be ready to answer on the spot.

BUILD THE BUSINESS CASE

QUESTIONS YOU SHOULD BE READY TO ANSWER ON APPOINTMENT

YOUR COMPANY

- How old is your company?
- What year was it founded?
- Where was it founded?
- Corporate headquarters?
- Regional headquarters?
- How many offices nationwide? Statewide? Internationally?
- Are you public? Which exchange is the stock traded? Symbol? Today's value?
- How many employees nationwide? Statewide? International? Total?
- How many salespeople nationwide? Statewide? International? Total?
- How are your divisions arranged? Who do you target? What areas do you target?
- Who is on the executive board? Who is the CEO/CFO/VP of sales?
- What is the mission statement?
- What is the website?
- Who does the company sponsor? Charities? Community Service?
- Where do they advertise?
- What are the contact numbers and e-mails of the sales manager, regional vice president of sales, director of sales, and customer service?
- What were revenues last year? Last quarter?
- What were revenues two years ago?
- Who are the biggest customers?
- What is the key to your company's success?
- Recent press releases? Recent media about your company?
- What else does the company sell outside of your division?
- What are your company's long-term plans? Revenue? Expansion? Products?

YOUR PRODUCT *(telecommunications is the example here)*

- How much does it cost? How much does each item cost?
- Package deal? Price good for how long?
- Month-to-month agreement/one-year/two-year/three-year commitment?
- Monthly/quarterly/annual commitment? Gross? Net?
- How long does it take to get it up and running? Delivered?

- Does the customer have to be there for delivery of your service?
- Will installation of your service interrupt the customer's current service? If so, for how long?
- Procedure for delivery?
- Twenty-four-hour customer service? Online?
- Who does the customer call if there is a problem initially?
- Price guarantee?
- Thirty-day window to return? Ninety-day window to cancel?
- Payment is due before delivery? Thirty days of delivery?
- One-year layaway plan?
- Does someone review my bill? Do you review my bill?
- Automatic renewal of agreement? You call me one month prior?
- What do I sign? Do I get a copy of it?
- What are the internal documents you hand in?
- Sample bill? Sample product?
- Instruction manual?

YOUR OWN INFORMATION

- How long have you been with your company?
- Why did you take the job?
- Where do you rank among the salespeople at your company?
- What has been the key to your success?
- Have you won any awards?
- Do you have any letters of recommendation? References?

- Hobbies?
- Long-term goals?
- What city do you live in? Family? Local organizations?
- What certification do you have?
- Are you involved in the community?
- How do you know So-and-So, who referred you to me?

So what is a personal profile? This is the way to humanize your business. This is the way to make the intangible tangible. The following page is an example.

TODD B. NATENBERG
President/Author
TBN Sales Solutions
5309 W. 153rd St., Leawood, KS 66224
Phone: (816) 876-9184
Todd@ToddNatenberg.com
www.IJustGotAJobInSales.com
www.toddnatenberg.com

Todd Natenberg, President of TBN Sales Solutions, increases commissions for salespeople through customized training. He establishes sales processes with private workshops, individual consulting and keynote speaking for associations to impact the bottom line.

Prior to the formation of TBNSS, Todd was a sales manager and regional sales trainer for Teligent, Inc., in Chicago, which offered local, long-distance, and data services nationwide. Previously, he was a top salesperson for LCI International, AT&T, USN Communications, and Canon, where he sold copiers. Todd also has worked as a district sales manager for Discovery Education.

His book, *"I just got a job in sales. Now what?" A Playbook for Skyrocketing Your Commissions* has been endorsed by notable experts including Brian Tracy, Roger Dawson, Stephan Schiffman, and Tony Parinello. His latest book, *"I've been in sales for 10 years! Now what?"*(Foreword by Roger Dawson) also received critical acclaim.

Todd recently produced, *How to Double Your Sales in ½ the Time: Sell How You Want to Buy*, a 10-hour interactive home study cd course.

He moved to Kansas City in 2007. He lives with his wife Reena and their amazing twin sons, Ari and Teddy in Leawood, Kansas.

SALES EXPERIENCE

TELECOMMUNICATIONS

ATT, LCI INTERNATIONAL, TELIGENT, USN COMMUNICATIONS

Sales Director, Regional Sales Trainer, Award-winning salesperson

EDUCATION

DISCOVERY EDUCATION, MEDICAST BY INVENTIVE TECHNOLOGY

District Sales Manager, Regional Sales Manager,

OTHER SALES POSITONS

CANON/AMBASSADOR OFFICE EQUIPMENT, CHERNIN'S SHOES

Sales Rep

JOURNALISM

THE ARIZONA REPUBLIC, KANSAS CITY STAR, CHICAGO DAILY HERALD, KANSAS CITY BUSINESS JOURNAL

Pulliam Fellowship, State/City Government Reporter, Utilities Reporter

COMMUNITY SERVICE

Ironman 2007 Finisher in Madison, WI in 16 hours, 30 minutes
Kansas City Junior Achievement Instructor
Former Chicago Junior Achievement Instructor
Society of Professional Journalists
Former Chicago/Kansas City Big Brother

PHILOSOPHY

> *"Customers do not care how much you know until they know how much you care. But showing how much you care includes showing how much you care about yourself.*
> *Sell how you want to buy."*

In terms of presenting, there are some specific things you need to be aware of. Now that we know what we are going to say, how are we going to say it? Even though you are not a public speaker, to succeed in sales, you need to speak well. Don't worry. If you weren't able to articulate well, you wouldn't have made it this far.

- *Be emotional.*

If you are a shy and quiet person, pretend you're not! You are in sales. You need to be excited about your product in order for others to be. If you don't believe in your product, who else will?

- *Mirror speech patterns of your prospect.*

As we discussed earlier, mimic your prospect as much as possible. While you need to be emotional and passionate, if the prospect is an analytical, slow talker, don't display an overwhelming energy level. Be enthusiastic, but in a different way.
Instead of talking fast, use gestures and smile.

- *Keep it simple, stupid.*

Even the most technical person wants a simple presentation. If you confuse the prospect, the sale is over. Don't make the prospect work. It's another recurring theme—simplicity.

> *It's a proven fact that the most technical buyers do not want a salesperson to be technical. They don't need an explanation of how it works technologically. They know that. They need you to tell them why they should care- how it's going to make their life easier.*

- *Interact*

It may be your turn to talk, but you must include your prospect in the presentation. To ensure that prospects are listening, engage them in the discussion. Check that they are acknowledging, repeating, and taking action based on what you say. Some great ways to interact without losing control include: Making eye contact with prospects, and asking the questions "what do you think so far?" or "does this make sense?"

> *Ninety-five percent of the time, prospects only find you pushy if they aren't interested. Asking once for an order is professional. Asking twice is persistent. Yes, three times is pushy. But if they are annoyed after the first or second request, they were annoyed from the onset.*

- *Place handouts directly in front of prospects*

When prospects can see and feel your presentation, they connect more with you and your product. This touches their own emotions, an essential element of the buying process. If you have a computer and are moving around a website, let them drive

- *Tie back to create those alignments*

You spent lots of time asking great questions. Use the information. Whenever possible, reference the past conversation. It proves you listened. Build those alliances. You might say, "Like you told me earlier about your company's success being based on great customer service, the same can be said for our company."

- *Trial close*

Trial closing is the strongest way to interact with prospects. It's also a great way to ultimately close the deal. Trial closing involves gathering prospects' buy-in along the way. Encourage "yes" to be their only response at the end, because they've been busy "yessing" along the way. Trial closes enable deals to close themselves.

The following are good questions to ask at the appropriate times:

- **"How will this help you?"**
- **"How much money will that save you?"**
- **"How much time will that save you?"**
- **"How many more hours a day will that give you?"**
- **"How will that help employee morale?"**

Closing a sale is like an algebra formula. If A=B and B=C, then A=C. If the prospect agrees with A, and A=yes, and if the prospect agrees with C, and C=yes, then yes=yes.

- *Transitions to stay on track.*

Don't turn the presentation into a one-way conversation, but do stay on track. Transitions are helpful. Address prospects' comments and questions as you go, but stay focused.

If a prospect wants to know the price, there is nothing wrong with saying, "We will get to that in a moment. Bear with me." If the prospect gets impatient, give a quick answer and return to your topic.

Likewise, if the prospect seems bored by your presentation, address it. Don't wait until the end. Your instincts are probably correct. Never talk about price until the very end.

Once the prospect appears to be on board, summarize the benefits of what you outlined again. Then ask for questions.

If prospects say they understand and you are confident it all looks good, now it's time to discuss the "investment opportunity you are inviting your prospect to participate in."

The key to addressing price successfully is to be matter-of-fact. If you have done your job properly, the prospect should be so excited that price is irrelevant.

Expensive is only expensive if it does not satisfy a need. There is price and then there is cost. Sell cost.

- *If the prospect is ready to buy, stop talking- and close*

Don't talk yourself out of a deal. If all goes as planned, the prospect will cut you off and sign the deal right there. Does this always happen? Of course not. But sometimes when prospects are ready to buy, salespeople insist on finishing their presentations.

They finish their presentations, but they frequently lose the deal.

- *Summarize one more time*

You have presented a lot of great information. You have spoken well. All information is important, but people remember most what they hear last. Don't expect the prospect to remember everything you've said. Simplify it. Here's how:

"So, Prospect So-and-So, our programs will address all your needs: customer service, billing, and the overall quality of what you are looking for. These were all things you mentioned that were important to you. Do you have any questions?"

I know there are still the big questions of what the investment is, but setting that aside for a moment, does everything else meet your needs?"

8. Close

There is no easier step in the sales process, but there is no scarier step. What's the worst that can happen? The prospect says no? No, the worst scenario is that the prospect wants to "think about it."

In our everyday personal lives, don't most of us want closure—good or bad? Uncertainty drives us crazy. Selling is no different. The good news is that if you have followed the process properly and you have made it to this point, the odds are greatly in your favor.

How do we close? Many books have been written on the subject. Indeed, many have been written, as well, about how not to close. Let's focus here on proper ways, rather than the improper. Don't beat around the bush. Just be direct.

Here's suggested wording, but really it's what works for you:

- "So, Prospect So-and-So, that's how it works. What do you think?"

- "So, Prospect So-and-So, it sounds good to me. Would you like to try us out?"

- "So, Prospect So-and-So, what do you think? Should we process the paperwork?"

- "So, Prospect So-and-So, when should we schedule delivery?"

- "So, Prospect So-and-So, all I need is your signature right here, and we'll get you going."

The key components to closing are:

☐ *Unshakable confidence*

You must believe that if you were on the other side of the table, you would buy your services, right then and there. One reason some reps have a tough time closing is because of their own buying habits. You cannot ask someone for an order and expect them to purchase if you really know that you personally would not buy at that moment.

If you would not purchase your own product at that moment, you will be unable to ask your prospect for the order.

Prospects can sense if you don't believe in what you are offering. They will tell themselves, "If the salesperson doesn't think I should buy, then I probably shouldn't."

Let's explore this a little further.

I recently had a conversation with a friend of mine who sold medical devices for a short period of time but now is in project management. He told me how he wasn't good at sales because he was too "honest." "I wasn't good, because I just couldn't lie to my customers. I had to tell them our problems."

Geez! Look, friends, just because a product has problems or a company has problems doesn't mean they shouldn't exist. It doesn't' mean you can't still help people and provide substantial value.

Contrary to some ill-conceived perceptions, prospects know they aren't buying perfection. That's why they have you. So if you know delivery will take longer than the prospect – or you wants- no big deal. Here's how it sounds:

Prospect: **"I need this to arrive in one month. Can that happen?"**

Salesperson: **"Of course, we will do our best, but for us to provide the necessary value and do this right, it probably will be at least 2 months."**

Prospect: **"I can live with that."**

It happens much easier than you think.

If customer services aren't 24/7, just tell them. What you consider objections, customers often don't. We will talk more about that later. Just know that if you really don't believe at all in what you are selling, find a different product, company or even career.

> *Perfection is the lowest standard of achievement. Why? Because nothing is perfect. If you strive for perfection, you will always fail.*

☐ *Silence*

Ask and be as quiet as a mouse. If you speak, you could blow the deal. Don't interrupt the prospect's train of thought. Silence is deafening, but it's a very powerful tool. Silence means prospects are thinking. It means they are thinking about why to buy your services. They are justifying the purchase in their minds.

☐ *Preparation*

Have paperwork filled out ahead of time. It shows your organizational skills and confidence. Remember the importance of simplicity. The easier it is to buy, the greater the likelihood they will. Here is another type of close.

"I'll tell you what. It sounds like there might be an opportunity here for us to help. Since we are both here now, why don't we sign the paperwork? I will call you in two days. If you decide against it, I will rip up the paperwork. This way, though, we can work by phone. You know integrity is everything to me. If I turned in an order without your authorization, I'd be fired."

This close often works, but you must be comfortable with it. It's not for everyone. I've used it many times in my career, and often prospects have signed. Statistically, when I've called back two days later, 90 percent of the time there are no problems. There have been maybe five times out of 100 when prospects have told me to rip it up. I have, and our relationships are all the stronger.

This close is recommended, because it gives you a measure of the level of the prospects' real interest. When prospects say, "It sounds great. I know we're going to do it. Just give me a couple days," sometimes the prospect is not being completely open. Sometimes the prospect is outright lying.

In these cases, one of the best strategies is to challenge. Challenge hard. You don't want to upset the prospect because often a sale occurs one, two, three months, or even a year later.

However, you don't want to spin your wheels unnecessarily. By challenging, you will find out where you truly stand.

A good, non-threatening way to measure a prospect's level of interest after an "I don't know" comment or a "give me a couple days" comment is to request a commitment to another appointment to sign the paperwork. If the prospect agrees, let go of the idea of closing the sale at that moment. You have done your job. You can leave feeling comfortable that you stand a good chance to get the deal at the next meeting.

If the prospect won't sign and won't commit to a timeframe, try a different tactic.

With unshakable confidence, say:

"Prospect So-and-So, let me ask you up front: I know when I'm not interested in something, I say the same thing: 'I'm not sure. Call me next week.' If that's what you are saying, I respect that, and we can part friends. But I don't want to waste your time or mine. They are equally valuable. Is that what you are telling me?"

The answer might be, "Yes, that's what I'm saying." If it is, then congratulations. You now know to move on. But most times, prospects will defend themselves. "No, I just need more time. I really am interested. Honest."

So what did we learn about building your business case?

1. Confirm appointment (but not how you think)

2. Wait like a pro

3. Set the agenda

4. Probe

5. Summarize

6. Present

7. Close

Closing is the easiest step in the process. It's opening the doors that are the challenge. Rather than closing a deal, open a relationship.

CHAPTER 7:

Follow Up

Follow-up: An organized system involving e-mail, phone calls and ongoing correspondence that is performed after the initial meeting

Selling is putting you in the right place at the right time to meet the right needs. Hard work is disguised as good luck.

Buyers rarely contact salespeople to ask for their services when they need them, even those with whom they have terrific relationships. The reason is not that they don't value you as a consultant. It's just that what exactly are "needs?" Food, shelter, and water are the only things humans truly need to survive. We want everything else.

Does a company really need better phone service? Does a controller really need to purchase new office equipment? Do CEOs need to impact the bottom line of their organizations? When buyers tell you, "We will call you if we need you," they are usually saying they aren't interested. Even when they determine they do want your services, they still may not call.

When a contract with their current vendor expires, buyers need a certain service. Indeed, they may even be unhappy with their current vendor and want to hire another vendor. But will they call *you*? How companies determine which organizations they need is often based on how you follow up.

A great example of this came early in my telephone career with my client, Matt. Then a prospect, Matt told me in June to call him around the holidays, knowing his agreement with his current provider would expire at that time. I called, and as a result, he bought my services.

"I'm just curious, Matt," I commented as he signed the paperwork. "Your agreement with the current vendor was due to expire, but if I hadn't contacted you, would you have contacted me? After all, you said you were interested and there was a need."

"Absolutely not," Matt answered. "Had you not called me, I would have just renewed our current agreement."

"Even though ours was clearly a better deal?" I asked.

"Yes, Todd," Matt said. "What earned you this deal was that you knew the difference between persistence and insistence."

> *Persistence is the ultimate compliment. Insistence is the ultimate deal killer.*

In this chapter, we will discuss the procedure for following up:

1. **E-mail everyone a summary thank you letter three days after the initial meeting**

2. **Update regularly**

3. **Refer business to prospects**

4. **Send monthly newsletter**

FOLLOW UP

1. E-mail everyone a summary thank you letter three days after the initial meeting

> *Interested prospects read your e-mail in their entirety-whether you are aware. They do care what you have to say, so long as it has value.*

Handwritten, mailed thank-you letters used to be special. They showed that salespeople took a personal interest in their customers. Unfortunately, handwritten notes do other things as well: They show messy often unreadable handwriting, take time to arrive at the destination, and have no electronic tracking.

People live through e-mail. When you e-mail information to people who actually want to correspond with you, it simplifies your life—and theirs. We've all spoken with people who say, "I know I have that information somewhere. Let me check my e-mail."

Another great thing about e-mail is it can be forwarded easily. In today's market, so many projects contain multiple decision makers and selling to various levels in an organization. When other people are brought into accounts, forwarding e-mail to bring them up to date is huge! You can't forward a handwritten letter.

> *Time is money – for both you and your prospects. Even if you have been successful with handwritten notes, know you could be that much MORE successful with e-mail thank you notes, when done properly.*

Thank anyone you meet in a formal appointment, networking event, or informal conversation via e-mail. Don't limit e-mail to those who need your services right now. Add everyone to your database. Often sending thank-you letters to prospects who say no to your services initially may get you the deal in the end simply because you were the only one to follow up. The above scenario with Matt was a prime example.

Also, remember the power of referrals. Even though a prospect may not directly be a candidate for your services, they may know someone who could benefit from meeting you. Following up professionally separates you from the pact.

In terms of my three day rule, for all you naysayers who say you should do it the day of, allow me to elaborate. Even with this fast pasted technology, I still strongly believe you wait three days. Here's why.

Think of your own attention span, for a moment. When you have a great conversation with people, after you leave them, you often need to digest what was spoken about. Don't you?

If you send e-mail to a hot prospect that day or the next day, individuals receiving them are impressed you sent the thank you right away. But they won't read it. They will merely see your name, assume it's a thank you and glance or delete it.

By the second day, you are a little bit off their radar but if you send it then, the same philosophy is that they may read a little bit but they think they know what was spoken, so they don't need to see it again.

Ah, but the third day? Now, they have moved on to other things. So when they receive an e-mail from you, it's the old, "Aha!" moment. They recognize your name and want to remember what the blazes you all discussed. This is where you get to control the conversation. How cool is that!

> *If the latest statistic says that it takes seven touches to get a prospect to buy, then if you send that e-mail the first or second day, it's like you blew one of the touch opportunities. But by waiting until the third day, you are actually lowering those seven necessary touches.*

So what should this three day later e-mail entail? Ironically, it will include three critical factors:

- *Summarize conversation*
- *Confirm commitments*
- *List next steps*

> *E-mail is to be used for accountability and marketing, never ever, never ever communication.*

E-mail holds everyone accountable. It ensures that you and your prospects are on the same page. Remember how real things become when they are written down? By summarizing, confirming and listing next steps, you advance the sale.

If you have a follow-up appointment, reference it. If you do not, but you have a timeframe, reference that. If there is no interest and it's a "down the road" situation, confirm it. Personalize the letter.

Remind prospects of their needs and how you offered to help. Include a written solution or your electronic brochure, or web link, even if they already have the hard copy.

> *The more you can organize your prospects, the easier you make their lives. The easier you make their lives, the more they will buy from you, because you are more than a salesperson. You are a true sustaining resource.*

The following pages include sample follow-up letters. The letters differ depending on the type of meeting and its result.

FIRST APPOINTMENT E-MAIL THANK YOU LETTER

Subject: Thanks for meeting in person; Follow up and next steps

So-and-So,

Thanks very much for meeting with me last week to discuss ways to skyrocket sales for your company. I appreciate the consideration.

Here's a summary of our discussion and next steps:

1. Your company has been successful because you provide top notch services and are dedicated to helping your clients in a consultative capacity.
2. Your biggest challenges from a sales training perspective are in the areas of prospecting, overcoming objections and having an overall sales process.
3. To help the process, I've enclosed electronic links to those above customized training programs you are most interested in....
4. Our next steps are as such:

    a. You, me, the VP of Sales, and your sales team will meet on Jan. 10 at 1:30 p.m.
    b. At that meeting we will further evaluate what's important to them in the areas outlined above.

Did I miss anything?

I appreciate the opportunity to help.

Sincerely,
Todd B. Natenberg

Author of, *"I've been in sales for 10 years! Now what?" A (NEW) Playbook for Skyrocketing Your Commissions*

Endorsed by Brian Tracy, Roger Dawson and Stephan Schiffman

President, TBN Sales Solutions

Phone: (816) 876-9184
e-mail: todd@toddnatenberg.com
http://www.toddnatenberg.com
www.ijustgotajobinsales.com

TBN Sales Solutions increases commissions for salespeople through customized training. We establish step-by-step sales processes with private workshops, individual consulting and keynote speaking for associations to impact the bottom line.

"Customers do not care how much you know until they know how much you care. But showing how much you care includes showing how much you care about yourself. Sell how you want to buy."

There are several things to note in this e-mail that have evolved in the 10 years since our original book was published. In the old days, the subject would be some benefit like: "Skyrocketing Sales…"

This is a different world. Remember you have relationships with these people. When we discuss follow up, we are not talking about follow up with suspects to make them into prospects. We are referencing real prospects. We are referencing either scheduled appointments that took place or at least face to face extensive discussions, such as a formal networking event or even an informal but complete conversation.

They recognize your name. They recognize your company. They do care what you have to say. So by saying, "Thanks for meeting in person," you remind them they know you and this is not just another cold call.

In addition, the "Thanks for meeting in person," keep you and they organized. When you need to reference past conversations, it serves as funnel management where you and them both can just type in the e-mail search engine, "in person" to find the correspondence.

SECOND APPOINTMENT (PROPOSAL) E-MAIL THANK YOU LETTER

Subject: Thanks again for meeting with me; Looking forward to finalizing our services

So-and-So,

I just wanted to drop you a quick note to say thanks again for chatting with me about a potential partnership between XXX and TBN Sales Solutions. I'm excited to work with your salespeople to start increasing commissions.

Per our conversation, I'm looking forward to meeting with you next on Jan. 20 at 1:30 p.m. At that time—if all is a go—we will sign the necessary paperwork and schedule dates for training.

I also have enclosed our solution electronically for your convenience. I thought you'd find it helpful.

I look forward to seeing you on January 20. Thanks again for the opportunity.

Sincerely,
Todd B. Natenberg

Author of, *"I've been in sales for 10 years! Now what?" A (NEW) Playbook for Skyrocketing Your Commissions*

Endorsed by Brian Tracy, Roger Dawson and Stephan Schiffman

President, TBN Sales Solutions

Phone: (816) 876-9184
e-mail: todd@toddnatenberg.com
http://www.toddnatenberg.com
www.ijustgotajobinsales.com

TBN Sales Solutions increases commissions for salespeople through customized training. We establish step-by-step sales processes with private workshops, individual consulting and keynote speaking for associations to impact the bottom line.

"Customers do not care how much you know until they know how much you care. But showing how much you care includes showing how much you care about yourself. Sell how you want to buy."

UNDECIDED/NO INTEREST E-MAIL THANK YOU LETTER

Subject: Thanks for meeting with me in person; Follow up and next steps

So-and-So,

Thanks very much for meeting with me last week to discuss ways to skyrocket sales for your company. I appreciate the consideration.

Per our conversation and my previous discussion with John Smith of Company XYZ who originally referred me to you, I am confident that after your evaluation you will agree we offer the best programs in today's sales training industry.

Naturally, I'm disappointed there is not more of an immediate opportunity to help. However, one thing I have learned in business is that what is not an opportunity today could always be one tomorrow. All I ask is that should your situation change, you will keep TBN Sales Solutions in mind.

Per your request, I will follow up with you in one month. In the interim, should anything change, please keep me posted.

Also, should you hear of any companies looking for top-notch sales training, please feel free to pass along my name and materials. To reiterate, my ideal client is:

- Fifty to five hundred employees
- 10 to 100 salespeople
- $5 million–$100 million in annual revenues
- Outside salespeople who call on accounts in person
- Multiple locations with headquarters in a major city
- Salespeople have never had formal sales training
- Company is at least 10 years old
- Decision maker is VP of Sales/CEO

- Technology company
- Telecommunications company
- Printers/web designers/graphics company
- Realtors (100 percent commissions)
- Mortgage Brokers (100 percent commission)
- Financial Planners (100 percent commission)
- Insurance Agents (100 percent commission)
- Network marketers (100% commission)
- One person entrepreneurs

Who can you refer me to?

Thanks again for the consideration. I look forward to speaking with you in two months.

Sincerely,
Todd B. Natenberg

Author of, *"I've been in sales for 10 years! Now what?" A (NEW) Playbook for Skyrocketing Your Commissions*

Endorsed by Brian Tracy, Roger Dawson and Stephan Schiffman

President, TBN Sales Solutions

Phone: (816) 876-9184
e-mail: todd@toddnatenberg.com
http://www.toddnatenberg.com
www.ijustgotajobinsales.com

TBN Sales Solutions increases commissions for salespeople through customized training. We establish step-by-step sales processes with private workshops, individual consulting and keynote speaking for associations to impact the bottom line.

"Customers do not care how much you know until they know how much you care. But showing how much you care includes showing how much you care about yourself. Sell how you want to buy."

A couple things I'd like to mention about the above letter to send when prospects aren't interested. You may think this is wordy, as well as a waste of time. But realize this may be the last correspondence you have with this prospect. Why not make it count?

You make thinking asking for referrals to someone who has not purchased your services and never may is bold, but so what? What do you have to lose? You aren't being rude or even pushy, just direct.

They may find you so professional, this letter could be the one that changes their mind. I have had too many clients to list here where I did not get the business the first time, but by being professional in rejection, I received it the second time. This strategy played an integral role.

Let me illustrate a case in point.

One of my best sales training clients was Wadsworth Pumps- in Arlington Heights, Illinois. They invested in sales training with me after purchasing phone services in both my LCI and USN Communications days. But at LCI, way back when, the first go around, they did not purchase from me.

But I kept in touch, and low and behold AT&T who they originally went with, did not meet their expectations. They actually broke their AT&T contract, switched to LCI through me, then USN through me after contracts expired, and ultimately TBN Sales Solutions. All this was because I followed up in rejection using the written word of e-mail.

2. Update regularly

Organizing yourself in the follow-up process is critical to success. Just because prospects aren't interested today, doesn't mean they won't be interested tomorrow. But if salespeople don't update prospects on a regular basis, they can miss out. Have a system for updating.
- Schedule the date and time to follow up in your electronic calendar.
- Treat updating as an appointment and stick to it
- Following up via e-mail, texting or phone is all acceptable in todays' technology world.

Let's take a moment to talk about how to actually provide that update in the various capacities.

- Phone

You must leave a voice mail on the direct line if the person you are trying to reach is not in. We discussed earlier the importance of leaving messages to give prospects reasons to call you back. Now leave messages to alert prospects you are honoring your commitment.

In other words, when prospects tell you to follow up with them on a certain day or month, let them know your word is gold. You'd be amazed at how many prospects are aware of who follows up and who doesn't.

Here's a recommended message to leave:

"Hello, Prospect So-and-So. This is Todd Natenberg, TBN Sales Solutions, (816) 876-9184. Sorry I missed you. I promised I'd follow up with you today, and I always follow through on my commitments. I just wanted to check in to see where we are and what questions you have. Again, Todd Natenberg (816) 876-9184.

- Texting

Ten years ago, getting a prospect's private cell phone number was unheard of. But times have changed. It says a lot about your relationship if they are willing to give you their cell phone. If they do, what are they saying? They are saying they invite you to contact them- however their cell phone operates. Texting is a huge part of cell phones today.

So what does a text say with the update? Keep it short and sweet. Suggested wording:

"Hi So-and-So. It's Todd Natenberg, TBN Sales Solutions. Just checking in? Any updates on us helping you?"

Other ways to update regularly include sending new articles about your industry, their industry, new products or promotions. You can send it via e-mail or fax.

(Fax is so outdated that it can actually work. More people read the fax now than ever before, because no one does it! It's worth trying! On the cover sheet, say this:

"FYI—I thought this would help your business." Todd

If you are huge fan of sending written mail, you will like this next recommendation. There is one time you can send something through the mail: Holiday cards. Once a year, I send a holiday card to my best prospects. I include my business card and make it personal. If you know when their birthday, do an electronic card via e-mail. It's just as personal.

3. Refer business to prospects

We will talk more about this in the networking chapter, but one of the best ways to earn business is to refer business. Even if nothing comes of it, prospects appreciate that you were thinking about helping them even *before* they paid you money for your services. It truly shows how much you do care about them as individuals. Referrals mean you want to develop relationships, not close deals.

But when referring business, it's important you follow a systematic formula. This helps your prospect, the person to who you are referring them, and yourself. It's a true win/win/win.

Here's what you do:

1. Don't just give your prospects the contact information and tell them to call another person.
2. Likewise, don't just give the person to who you are referring the prospects' information.

3. Send e-mail to all parties involved making it clear that everyone is getting a referral that will help their business. (Remember, referrals aren't just about increasing revenues for one party. The person receiving valuable service is just as appreciative).

SAMPLE GIVING REFERRAL E-MAIL

Subject: Referral for John at Company ABC and Steve at Company DEF; Increasing both your revenues

John and Steve,

I have a referral for both of you.

(John, Susie is a terrific business manager with XXX. She is an old running friend. I have not spoken with her in a while. However, I think your business could greatly help hers. It's certainly worth a phone conversation).

(Susie, it's your old running buddy, Todd Natenberg. I hope all's well. John is the owner of XXX. They work closely with hospitals to improve performance through customized phone solutions. I'd highly recommend you consider her services. Either way, she's someone you should know.)

Here's everyone's contact information:

John
Company XXXX
(555) 555-5555
Kansas City, Missouri
john@1234.com

Susie
Company XXX
(555) 555-5555
Susie@3456.com

Please call me at (816) 876-9184 or e-mail with questions.

Good luck to all! Please keep me posted.

Sincerely,
Todd B. Natenberg

Author of, *"I've been in sales for 10 years! Now what?" A (NEW) Playbook for Skyrocketing Your Commissions*

Endorsed by Brian Tracy, Roger Dawson and Stephan Schiffman

President, TBN Sales Solutions

Phone: (816) 876-9184
e-mail: todd@toddnatenberg.com
http://www.toddnatenberg.com
www.ijustgotajobinsales.com

TBN Sales Solutions increases commissions for salespeople through customized training. We establish step-by-step sales processes with private workshops, individual consulting and keynote speaking for associations to impact the bottom line.

"Customers do not care how much you know until they know how much you care. But showing how much you care includes showing how much you care about yourself. Sell how you want to buy."

4. Send monthly newsletter

If people continually complain they are repeatedly bombarded with promotions and other forms of e-mail marketing then why do electronic newsletters still exist? It's because they work. They are convenient. They don't take up paper space, and readers can forward the material to others. In addition, they again facilitate record keeping.

To make the most out of your electronic newsletter, it must be valuable to prospects.

Give *free* information relevant to your product and industry that, if utilized, will impact the bottom line for your prospects. This keeps your name in front of the prospect and further establishes you, the salesperson, as a true consultant who is an asset to impact their bottom line.

To deciding what to include in your newsletter, simply ask yourself if you were your client/prospect in their industry, would what you are providing them help them? Ask yourself the following:

- If they use the information you provide, will it reduce their cost in some area?
- Will it increase their revenues in some areas?
- Will it improve their efficiency?

For example, since I provide customized sales training service, my newsletter may have free sales tips about how best to prospect. Back in my Discovery days, when I sold online educational K-12 curriculum, I provided tips about how best to improve teaching performance.

What other content can you potentially included in newsletters?

- Industry articles to keep prospects up to date on the latest and greatest in your field
- Articles about your company or product, specifically ones that appear in other publications (or perhaps your own internal newsletter)
- New promotions or products at your company.

The best place to acquire these materials is by subscribing to electronic newsletters or scouring the internet through keyword searches. LinkedIn groups also are terrific. In addition, sending these articles are very easy utilizing "cut and paste" features.

So what did we learn about follow up?

1. **E-mail everyone a summary thank you letter three days after the initial meeting**

2. **Update regularly**

3. **Refer business to prospects**

4. **Send monthly newsletter**

Selling is about how many times you can get in front of how many opportunities in how many ways to communicate valuable information.

CHAPTER 8:

Overcome Objections

> Objections: Buying signals in which emotions are expressed.

If a prospect's concern can't be overcome by you or another vendor, it is not an objection. Before you address it, determine what it is you are addressing.

People buy on emotion. Think of your own buying habits. When was the last time you made a significant purchase and did not ask a single question? When was the last time you bought, but did not voice any concerns?

Take it one step further. When was the last time you were uninterested in an item but asked questions about it? People only have concerns if they are interested, if there is something about which to be concerned.

A while back, I bought a five-bedroom house with a walk-out finished basement with my wife, Reena, here in Kansas. Prior to purchasing, we examined other potential properties. We asked nothing about those in which we had no interest. These homes either did not meet our geographical needs, were not the size we wanted or for whatever reason did not on the surface meet our criteria.

There was no point in discussing these matters because nothing could be done about these issues. They were what they were.

But prior to taking out a mortgage on the home we were interested in, we asked many questions. They ranged from the quality of the neighborhood and schools to the nearest grocery store to what is the reason the current owners are moving. Even the question about homeowner dues (a money question!) only came up if the other criteria seemed to be met.

My realtor helped me overcome these objections by tapping into our emotions, but only because I let him. He was only able to because my wife and I expressed our emotions. One by one, he addressed each concern with us. One by one, together we converted fear into excitement. Notice my wording. *Together-* we overcame our objections. That is the only way this works.

> *If prospects think you are overcoming their objections, you are done for. If they view you as working with them to overcoming their objections, that's a partnerships. Partnerships produce sales.*

In this chapter, we will present the playbook for overcoming objections.

1. **Pause**

2. **Empathize**

3. **Probe**

4. **Playback**

5. **Solve**

1. Pause

When a prospect expresses a concern, do nothing. Don't respond. Count to ten in your head slowly. Then say, "Hmmm" but nothing else.

Recognize that what was spoken is still only a concern. It's not yet an objection. Maybe the prospect is thinking out loud. The prospect could be talking for the sake of talking. You don't know what is going through the prospect's mind. How often have you blurted out comments with no intention of getting a response?

It's vital you don't interrupt your prospect's thought process. Thinking takes work. Having to think again takes even more work. If your prospect is willing to work to buy your services, you're in.

> ***Silence means they are thinking about why to buy your service, not why not to buy. If they did not want to buy, they'd just say so. Stay in silence.***

In addition, if you speak too quickly, you will often come across as defensive. If you start defending yourself, you just validated their concern. If you had said nothing, the whole issue may have subsided and may not even have needed to be addressed.

Compare selling with the role of parents watching their child fall down. Now, I love my wife, Reena more than anything in this world. She is a great wife and super mom. But I have to say that when it comes to Ari and Teddy (who are four year old twin boys at the time of the writing of this book), as a loving mother, sometimes her overprotectiveness does get the best of her. If Ari or Teddy falls down playing basketball, baseball or tennis, sometimes she will rush over in a panic to see they are okay. They had no intention of crying until they saw Reena's reaction.

Of course, I love my sons likewise more than anything and don't want them hurt. But I do pause myself to examine what really happened. I can't validate their crying until I know that it is real and not a "cry wolf" as we say.

If they are hurt and cry, I make a "safe" sign, like a baseball umpire does in making a call. I do it with a smile and they laugh. Sometimes, the "safe" sign is made even when I know they are hurt and we may even need to go to the hospital. It keeps everyone calm in what could be a tense situation.

How they react often is based on how Reena and I react. The world of sales is no different.

In my telecommunications days, more than one conversation like the following occurred:

Prospect: "It sounds good, Todd. But six cents a minute is more than I was hoping to pay."

Me: Pause.
Me: Pause.

Prospect: "But I guess it's a good price. I'm still saving money. Let's do it."

2. Empathize

If you have paused, but the prospect is still looking at you, waiting for you to say something, now it's your turn to respond.

Note: If you are on the phone, wait for the prospect to literally say, "Did you hear me? Are you there?" It's a great strategy.

Don't argue, but don't validate the comment in its entirety at this point. Think of that parent's reaction to the child. Show you understand. Communicate to prospects that their concerns are valid, but not valid enough to not buy. In sales circles, this is known as "feel, felt, found."

Here are the words to use:

"I understand how you feel, Prospect So-and-So. Other clients of ours have felt the same way. But what they have found after

OVERCOME OBJECTIONS

purchasing our services is that they made the right decision going with us."

3. Probe

If you still have not defused the situation with pause, relax, and empathize, now you should ask questions to assess the situation. Make sure you understand what was spoken. What you think you heard and what the prospect intended are not always the same.

What, exactly, is the concern? What is the objection? Is it even an objection that can be overcome?

Probing is important because it puts concerns into one of three categories: statements, deal- and objections.

- *Statements*

Part of the definition of "objection" is that emotions must be expressed. A statement does not express emotions. Talking is not an emotion.

When you say "I don't know," that is not an emotion because you could mean "maybe" or "maybe not." This may be a funny example, but it's actually very relevant.

Did you ever see the motion picture, *Fast Times at Ridgemont High* in the 1980s starring Sean Penn.? There's a hysterical scene where the English teacher, Mr. Hand, played by Ray Walston, asked the Penn character (Jeff Spicoli), "Why Mr. Spicoli do you always waste my time?"

Spicoli: "I don't know."

Mr. Hand: "I don't know. I like that. Let's examine that statement. Gee, Mr. Hand. Will I pass English? Gee, Mr. Spicoli, I don't know! "

> **Indecisiveness is not an emotion. Happiness, sadness, and anger are emotions. Make sense?**

- *Deal breaker*

Ask yourself if your prospect's concern is one you can overcome with the perfect wording or the perfect solution. Is it realistic that if you are brilliant, you can comprise the perfect honest answer?

In telecommunications, I was in many situations where a prospect had a five-year contract with a $100,000 penalty if broken. My service would only save the prospect $1,000 overall. While stressing to never sell on price, a $100,000 penalty is a deal-breaker, unless I'm willing to make up the $99,000.

The challenge is determining whether something is truly a deal-breaker. What are the terms of the contract? Are there loopholes? Perhaps you could earn some of the business, but is it worth it? The key to addressing whether it is a deal breaker is to probe as previously stated.

> *The best salespeople I know recognize deal breakers as early in the process as possible. When they do, they gladly walk away.*

- *Objection*

How do we know when a concern is a legitimate objection? Certain criteria must be met.

- Emotion must be expressed—positive or negative.
- Specific, measurable issues must be voiced.
- The impact on the company's business must be real.
- There must be a clear solution—somewhere, somehow- if not by you and your company then another.

Overcoming objections is a form of negotiating. It is a win-win scenario. The goal is not to prove prospects wrong. The goal is to have prospects prove themselves wrong. Lead prospects to overcome their own objections. Let them make their own decisions, with help from you.

Asking lots of questions, followed by long periods of silence, helps accomplish this task. Some good questions to ask include:

- **"How do you mean?"**
- **"Oh, why is that?"**
- **"I don't understand. Please help me out."**
- **"Can you explain further? I'm confused."**

Let's talk about these last two about being confused and not understanding. In the old days, we called this strategy the *Columbo* theory, based on the hit television show starring Peter Falk in the 1970's. As ten years have passed, I now officially dub this the *Law and Order: Criminal Intent* theory.

In *Law and Order*, the Vince Vaughn lookalike actor (you know who I mean- Vincent D'Onofrio) plays detective Robert Goren. Goren always gets the suspect to confess, but not because he possesses brilliant, confrontational skills. It's the opposite. He always talks slowly, uses hand gestures, pulls his body back as to show sympathy, acts confused and always is just "trying to understand."

Here's an example of how he does it:

Detective Goren: "I'm a little confused. Can you *help* me understand? That doesn't make sense how you described it. I'm a little slow. I apologize."

Suspect: "Geez, What don't you get? I killed the person. Understand?"

Detective Goren: "Oh, I see...You are under arrest."

4. Playback

When you have enough information to judge whether this is a deal-breaker or an objection, repeat your understanding to the prospect. This does a few things:

- Ensures you and the prospect agree with what it is preventing you both from forging ahead
- Enables prospects to hear their own objections aloud.
- Proves you were listening to the prospect (as we described previously)

If what you repeat does not match up with what the prospect meant to say, prospects will appreciate your desire to clarify. Best of all, they will clarify it for you. As we said, when they state their own objection out load, that's key. Then they will know whether they have a legitimate concern or are just being nitpicky.

Here is an example:

You: "Okay, Prospect So-and-So. I think I understand what you are saying. The issue for you is not that things are fine as they are. You are questioning whether it's worth the additional cost to have better customer service with us.

"You agree our service could—if executed properly—save your company ten hours more per week, thereby impacting your bottom line greatly. But you question just how those ten additional hours will come about.

"In other words, you are not sure whether our overall value is worth it. If you agreed that we would save your company ten hours per week, then we could go ahead. Is that right?

Prospect: "Yes."

You: "So the real issue is will our service do what we say?"

Prospect: "Yes, I guess that's the issue. Why don't you walk me through it again?"

That's when you know you are very close to overcoming an objection. Why? Because now they are willing to work to convince themselves they want to purchase from you.

Playing back also avoids you creating self-imposed objections.

OVERCOME OBJECTIONS

We stated earlier that if you won't buy your own service, you can't sell it. The same theory is relevant to objections. If you think your price is too high, the prospect certainly will.

Too often, salespeople claim they are being honest by bringing up problems with their products or companies, even when the prospect doesn't actually have that concern. I will say it again that just because something isn't perfect doesn't mean you can't provide value.

This is another example why the veteran salespeople like yourself sometimes struggles but the rookie who "know nothing" does great.

> *Don't defend that which does not need defending. What's important to the prospect is what matters, not what's important to you. They should be one and the same.*

For instance, if prospects say they are concerned about customer service, don't lower the price. They did not say the price was too high. You did. Not only is altering the price not necessary, it's counterproductive. Prospects may become angry that you did not listen to their true concerns. They may walk away for that reason alone. If they don't walk away, you may have cost yourself and your company money unnecessarily.

There is no easier way to lose a sale than to prove to prospects you did not listen to their concerns. Never address an objection the prospect does not want addressed.

One of the most common ways to create self-impose objections is by being too technical. It's worth repeating: *Keep it simple.*

Consider again your own buying habits. If you are confused about something, how often will you ask for an explanation? If you are determined to buy an item at all costs, you will ask. But if you are on the bubble, more often than not, you won't waste time or energy.

No one wants to look foolish. Not only that, but if a seller talks over your head as a buyer, aren't you a little insulted? I know for me even if I want to purchase the product, if I become very irritated, I may even ask the manager to find me a new salesperson.

What a shame that would be if your company sold the product and you didn't get credit!

> *Make it easy for prospects to buy, and they will. Make it hard, and they won't.*

5. Solve

Solving an objection is similar to presenting on a sales call, only abbreviated. To overcome the objection, utilize your visuals once again. The reason why is that when a true objection surfaces, prospects usually doubt what you said. They question the validity of your offering. Show them that what you said is fact, not opinion, by using support materials. How do you do that?

Remember those great visuals you compiled for your pitch book? Let's return to that. Here it is once again:

EVERYTHING NEEDED TO OVERCOME OBJECTIONS

- Pen
- Pad of paper for notes
- Datebook (electronic or written)
- Business cards
- Pricing (all pricing)
- Contracts (necessary documents requiring signatures)
- Internal paperwork (demonstrating to customers what's required on your end)
- Product samples (either physical or pictures)
- Presentations (electronic or written)
- Testimonial letters about your company
- Testimonial letters about you
- Media articles about your company
- Media articles about your company's industry
- Color brochures about your company
- Color brochures about your product
- Written guarantees your company or product offers
- One-pager "What [Your Company] Can Do for You"
- One-pager company contacts
- One-pager personal profile
- One-page implementation schedule
- Print out of all e-mail correspondence between you and prospect to demonstrate commitments made

EXERCISE #O1—TOP 10 OBJECTIONS

1. Go into a room with open wall space.
2. If you are on a sales team, gather your colleagues and manager to conduct this exercise with you.
3. Gather ten big pieces of paper—eleven by twenty-four inches is great, but eight and a half by eleven inches is fine, too.
4. Tape each piece of paper to the wall.
5. Label each piece of paper "Objections" and number them one through ten.
6. Brainstorm the top ten objections you encounter in your daily job.
7. Decide which ones are statements, which are deal-breakers, and which are objections
8. Label them with an S, DB, or O.
9. Write down every response you can imagine to each.

The following pages list various suggested responses to common statements, deal-breakers, and objections, regardless of industry. History has proven the effectiveness of these scripts. Remember to use these scripts only after pause, relax, empathize, probe, and playback.

OBJECTION HANDLING SCRIPTS

- <u>"If it ain't broken, don't fix it."</u>

"I understand exactly how you feel. Several of my clients have felt the same way during our initial discussions. But what they have found after speaking with us is that keeping things as they are does not always provide a solution that could grow their business. What we are talking about is a way to further impact your bottom line. What could the company do with this extra money? Isn't that a reason right there to improve the situation?"

- <u>"I need references."</u>

"I don't mind giving you references, but before we do that, I want to make sure we have all our bases covered. Just like if you were my customer and I used you as a reference, I wouldn't want to bombard you with favor requests, such as phone calls from other opportunities until we have everything else ironed out. Does that make sense?

So let me ask you, is this the only thing standing between us and a new customer at this point?

"No? Then why don't we address the other issues first? Is that fair?"

- <u>"We don't have it in the budget."</u>

You: "How do you mean? Have it in the budget? Have what in the budget? Help me understand. I'm a little confused."

Prospect: "Your price is too high. I can get your services for less down the street."

You: "In what respect? My price? You mean you are worried you won't get the proper return on your investment? Help me out here."

Prospect: "Yes, that's right—my return on the investment. I'm just not sure the change is worth it."

You: "So the issue is not the price. You are questioning whether you will get the value you are looking for. You question whether we can deliver what we say? It's almost the 'too good to be true' situation?"

Prospect: "Yeah, I guess that's it."

You: "Well, let me explain our programs again."

- *"Your price is too high. I can get it for less somewhere else."*

You: "I'm a little confused. When we spoke earlier, you indicated that what were important to you were reliability and one point of contact. You said those were the concerns of yours that were not being addressed by your current vendor. Did I miss something? Please clarify for me.

"As I indicated earlier, we will never be the cheapest or the most expensive. Much like your business, we, too, have been successful because of our quality and service."

- *"Who are you? I've never heard of your company."*

You: "That's a fair question. I understand exactly how you feel. Several of my clients felt the same way during our initial discussions. But what they found out after speaking with us is that because we are not one of the "major players," we can provide unequaled personalized attention. Because we do not have as many customers as the larger companies, we must earn your business on a daily basis. That means I have to be head and shoulders above the rest. Much like your company, it's been the key to our success."

- *"We tried switching vendors before. It was a disaster. It's not worth the risk again."*

You: "You indicated that earlier, but it sounds like maybe we did not address it enough in depth. What specifically are you concerned would happen again? Help me understand."

Prospect: "The service went down. It cost us time and money, and we had nothing to show for it."

You: "So you question what we will do differently to ensure these problems don't repeat themselves?"

Prospect: "Yes."

You: "Okay, so what you are saying is that if you felt more comfortable that this would not happen, you'd be okay?"

Prospect: "Yes."

You: "I do understand how you feel. Several of my clients have felt the same way. What they have discovered—in the end—is that we delivered on our promises."

Prospect: "Still, I'm just not sure. Why don't you walk me through it again?"

- *"We used your company before. It was a disaster."*

You: "I am sorry to hear that. I offer no excuses. But let me ask you if you had the opportunity to earn back a customer's business you lost, wouldn't you want that?"

Prospect: "Sure."

You: "I do understand how you feel. Several other clients have felt the same way. What they have found out, after exploring our new services, is that we are a much better company now. In fact, it is because of those problems that my division was formed-: to correct those problems we once had. Can I get a shot at reestablishing your trust? Can you help me out?

- *"It sounds good, but my boss will never go for this."*

You [flinching, expression of surprise]: "Your boss? I'm a little confused. When we spoke, you indicated you were the one who signed on the dotted line. I apologize if I misunderstood you."

Prospect: "Well, I just have to run it by him."

You: "Okay. Well, if that's the case. I'll tell you what. Let's do a couple of things. Let's schedule an appointment with him, where you and I can position us together. What can you and I do to work as 'partners' to show him the benefits? If you were me, what would you recommend? Your ideas will really help me."

Prospect: [Answers.]

You: "Also, naturally one question he will ask you is if you were him, what would you do?"

Prospect: "Oh, if it were up to me, I'd do it."

You: "Terrific. Then my work is done—for the moment."

- *"We're bound by a contract."*

OVERCOME OBJECTIONS

(This is a tricky situation, where you need to see if they really are bound by a contract or it's just an excuse. Let's explore it).

You: "How do you mean?"

Prospect: "If we used you, we'd be penalized."

You: "Forget us for a moment. What are the terms of the agreement? When does it expire? Would there be an opportunity for you to try out a portion of our services?"

Prospect: "Yeah, I guess so—now that you mention it."

- *"There's no reason to do it now. Maybe later. I'll call you in two months."*

You: "Prospect So-and-So, we are both business people. I don't want to waste your time or mine. They are equally valuable. I know when I'm not interested in something, that's exactly what I say. If you're saying you're not interested, I'll respect that and I'll move on. Am I reading you correctly?"

Prospect: "No, not at all. I really am interested. It's just that later might be a better time. There's no rush."

You: "All right. Then, let me ask you an up-front question. Why would another time be better than now? What would change that would create this sense of urgency?"

Prospect: "I don't know. It's just we have a lot going on now. We don't have time to mess around with this."

You: "Oh, I see. So you are concerned that switching to us would be the equivalent of 'messing around,' and you are wondering what the repercussions would be if we did not deliver as promised?"

Prospect: "Yes, I suppose so."

You: "Well, in that case, let's review our programs again."

Prospect: "No, just call me in two months."

You: "Fair enough. The other thing I will share is that maybe our programs are not a good fit. That is possible. They are not for everybody. I'm confident we can help you, but in the end, your decision will be based on your gut feeling. No fancy brochure or even proven history will alleviate that concern. Maybe we aren't what you looking for."

Prospect: "Wait a second. I didn't say that. Let's reexamine this."

So what did we learn about objection handling?

1. Pause

2. Empathize

3. Probe

4. Playback

5. Solve

People buy on emotion. If emotions are not expressed, objections do not exist. If objections do not exist and a person does not buy at that moment, the sale will never be made.

CHAPTER 9:

Network

Networking: The developing of long-term relationships based on mutual exchange of information to help enhance the lives of at least two individuals.

Giving and receiving ideas to help improve one's own business, giving and receiving support to help improve one's attitude, and giving and receiving contacts to further position oneself as a sustaining resource are all networking.

Why are the best salespeople always the best networkers? It's because networking is more than swapping leads and closing deals, as is selling. Networking is building relationships based on mutual trust. It's two individuals helping one another to ultimately make more money through the exchange of information.

Networking does not involve companies. It involves individuals. When you network properly, both parties agree to dedicate themselves to helping one another, regardless of their companies.

More importantly, networking involves helping others first, then seeking help for yourself.

In this chapter, we will present the playbook for how to network:

1. Understand what it takes to network

2. Decide with whom to network

3. Know what to say when networking

4. Schedule formal "coffee" appointment – but be selective

5. Follow up via e-mail

6. Send PAL before the formal appointment

7. Conduct the appointment in a non-lunch atmosphere

8. Follow up with a 3-way referral

1. Understand what it takes to network

Everybody claims to network. But to network effectively, you must have a certain mindset that translates into executable behavior.

While your goal in reading this book is to make money for you and your company, the information you gain is yours. It will last you the rest of your life. The same can be said for networking.

When you leave your company, you will take your ideas, contacts, and networking relationships with you. It would be great to think you will stay at your company for the next 10 years, but the cold hard truth is that selling is a volatile profession. You are making an investment in reading this book, even if your company footed the bill.

Nothing is more valuable than time. It is the only thing we can control. Networking is just as personal, and time consuming.

To be the best networker, treat everybody you encounter like a prospect- in a terrific way. Give them the same respect, courtesy, and attention you would give those who may buy your services. Follow up with them regularly.

I know you may be asking yourself what kind of way is that to live if everyone you meet should be treated as a business opportunity. That's not what I'm saying. What I am saying though is with everybody you meet from here on you should ask yourself, "How can I help this person?" Now, isn't' that an awesome way to live?

> *"It is one of the most beautiful compensations of life that no man can sincerely try to help another without helping himself."* – **Ralph Waldo Emerson**

From an organization standpoint, you must incorporate networking directly into your weekly schedule, as discussed earlier. Know which days you will formally network through in person scheduled appointments and what events you will attend to find those prospects.

From a mindset standpoint, you must be willing to take the first step at events or while out and about. You need to approach others.

Don't wait for them to approach you. Bring up the issue to your friends at the fitness club. As you would with a prospect, share your "ideal client" criteria and ask new networking friends the ideal criteria for their clients. But be patient. Results take time. The more you give, the more you receive.

> *Persistence, patience and perseverance are the keys to success, the keys to life.*

2. Decide with whom to network

Earlier, we discussed the importance of identifying your ideal client. In networking, same rules apply. To make the most of networking, identify those who can help you the most—and those who you can help most. Usually, they are the same people.

Don't get caught up in the chamber of commerce or leads groups unless those people target the same accounts you target or represent the types of accounts you want as customers. Networking is dangerous because, if you aren't careful, you can get involved in making a lot of friends without generating a lot of opportunity.

It's not necessary to meet with everyone. If you are in doubt as to whether you and your new friend can help one another, it's worth erring on the side of meeting, but you still need to be selective. Even though everyone should be entered in your database, some people can help you more than others, just as there are people you can help more than others.

> *The person to network with is the person who has access to your ideal client, wants to connect you with that ideal client, and wants you to connect them with their deal client. Only then does everybody win.*

Here are some good questions to consider when deciding whether to grab that cup of coffee with someone to take it to the next level.

- Do they want to network with you?
- Do they target the same accounts as you?
- Do they have the same sales territory?
- Does their product complement yours (i.e., sales training company could network with strategic management company)?
- Do you feel comfortable referring business to them?

(Their actions are a direct reflection—positive or negative—on you. If you are concerned they will not follow up promptly, don't refer them business. Since you are a professional, it will be a poor reflection on you if you refer an amateur.)

- Do they feel comfortable referring you?
- Do they sell the same way as you?
  (Are they passive and calm? Or are they aggressive and persistent?)
- Do you have similar personality traits?
  (People network with people they like- and people like them).
- Are you similar in age?
- (Sometimes, this is good. Sometimes, it's not. Think about it.)
- Are your companies similar in size?
- Do you sell the same product but with different targets?
  (Competitors can be great sources as long as you target different size accounts.)
- Can you learn from them? Will they make you a better salesperson?

The following page suggests people with whom you might want to network. (Notice that it is almost the same list as those people with whom you would seek referrals.)

NETWORKING SOURCES

- Customers
- Prospects
- Friends/relatives
- Internal employees
- Vendors
- Office equipment vendor
- Office supplies vendor
- Your accountant
- Your attorney
- Your insurance agent
- Your local, long distance, cellular phone, web hosting, Internet provider
- Your health club
- Your landlord/condo association
- Your barber
- Your grocery store manager
- Your dry cleaner
- Members of associations in which you or company have memberships
- Members of chambers of commerce in which you or company have memberships
- Members of chambers of commerce in area in which you live (even without membership)
- High school and college alumni organizations
- Previous employers
- Past internal employees from previous employers
- Previous prospective employers
- Competitors
- Salespeople who sell to the same clients in the same territory, but with a different product
- Salespeople who sell a complimentary product in the same industry (e.g., phone equipment vendors referring phone service providers)

- Referral groups where leads are exchanged and membership often is paid
- LinkedIn contacts (first, second, third connections, groups, discussions)
- Other social media contacts (Facebook, Twitter, etc.)

3. Know what to say when networking

Once you know the kinds of people with whom you want to network, you need to create scripts to understand how to maximize your time with them. As part of this, recognize that there are two types of networking: formal versus informal.

Formal Networking

Formal networking occurs at official functions. These include association meetings, chamber of commerce luncheons, after-hours, and industry events. Everyone attends these events to make contacts. They can garner results, but they can be challenging. In essence, they are one big sales pitch. Everyone is selling everyone. The winner is usually the person who gives the most leads and asks the most questions.

Informal Networking

While attending formal networking events is important, informal networking is where you separate yourself from the pact. This includes asking for help and providing help to friends, family, other health club members, etc. It is often frightening because you must be proactive in initiating contacts.

It may sound challenging bringing up the business conversation in what appears a personal environment. But again, if your business is all about helping, what's wrong with that? So long as it is done tactfully and very genuinely, everyone wins.

Besides, think about the most common topics in life beyond family and friends. Aren't they politics, world affairs, sports and business? What's wrong with bringing up the last one since it's coming up anyway?

> *"There is no difference between what I do as a youth pastor helping people in a church and what you do as a salesperson helping people in the corporate world."*
> – Nate Severson, Hillcrest Cove, Overland Park, KS

Now that we've established the different kinds of networking, let's delve into the logistics of what you say.

☐ *Introduce*

How you introduce yourself will often determine whether a networking opportunity will be created. Whether in an informal or formal networking situation, get in the habit of introducing yourself in the following way:

- Firm handshake
- Smile
- Ask them their name
- Repeat their name; say your name

☐ *Probe*

One of the biggest differences between networking and prospecting is that when you network, you do not say what you do until other people ask. First, find out what they do. Ask questions. Like on sales calls, you will automatically endear yourself.

In addition, the more you probe, the more others want to not knowing what you do. You are so concerned about how you can help them that your own needs have become secondary. They see this. It will reach a point where they will say, "I'm sorry. We've been so busy talking about me. What do you do?" Here are suggested questions to ask before you even say what your job is:

- **"What do you do?"**
- **"What has been the key to your success?"**
- **"What's your biggest challenge?"**
- **"Who is the best client for you?"**

☐ *State Initial Benefit*

You've asked so many good questions that, at long last, the person with whom you are speaking can't wait to hear what you do. When that person asks, it's show time! You have this person's undivided attention. Now it's time for that amazing initial benefit statement. Never say, "I sell phone service." Give them your best initial benefit statement as you did back in the prospecting chapter. Then pause. Wait for a reaction.

Ideally, this person will ask more questions. Be careful, because this is your time to sell yourself. The best way to sell you is by making the conversation about them, not you. Answer all their questions, but relate them back to what they said when they shared information about their business. Like we discussed earlier, build alliances to tie them back later.

4. Schedule formal "coffee" appointment – but be selective

Effective networking is not completed in a two-minute conversation. It requires an extensive in-person discussion to learn more about one another and how you can help one another. When you think you have enough information about this individual and that you are in a position to mutually benefit, cease the conversation by politely saying you would like to talk more at another time.

If you don't think a future meeting would help further either of your businesses, politely excuse yourself. If it's a formal event, ask where the bathroom is, say that you'd like some food, or simply indicate you'd like to walk around.

But if you would like to get to know this person better, try to commit to a date and time right then and there. Pull out your datebook and schedule an appointment on the spot. Don't be too aggressive, but let them know you mean business.

But because you are not in a true prospect/salesperson setting, go with the coffee comment. You and the person you want to meet with will realize that the odds of you actually drinking coffee are less than 1%, but in this day and age, it works. Here's what you say:

"I think we are in a great positon to help one another. Want to meet for coffee and discuss it further?"

If you have the opportunity to avoid a possible game of phone tag, do so. If you just can't connect at that moment for whatever reason, follow up with phone and e-mail to schedule that meeting.

Let me take a moment to emphasize my "if beneficial" comment. Contrary to what you have been taught, you don't meet with everybody for that formal appointment.

Yes, you talk to all you can on the spot, but when it comes time for that formal appointment, return to the list of those you want to network closely with. You may not have all the answers in your five minute conversation, but do your best.

> *If you formally network with everyone you network with no one. Make friends to have fun. Network to make business.*

5. Follow up via e-mail

Whether you want to go to the next level of formal networking in an actual meeting, always send e-mail to those you have a significant conversation with in networking. Remind them via e-mail, including attachments with your basic company information, and web link, as outlined earlier. The following pages have various templates to help.

NETWORKING/WANT TO MEET FOLLOWUP E-MAIL

Subject: Basketball friend/TBN Sales Solutions President says great meeting you in person

So-and-So,

It was great meeting you recently at the ZZZ. I'm looking forward to helping one another.

Per our discussion, I have enclosed the benefits on my company, TBN Sales Solutions- and how we increase commissions for salespeople through customized training.

After you have had a chance to review the materials, I'd welcome grabbing coffee to discuss how we can help one another.

To reiterate, my ideal client is:

- Fifty to five hundred employees
- 10 to 100 salespeople
- $5 million–$100 million in annual revenues
- Outside salespeople who call on accounts in person
- Multiple locations with headquarters in a major city
- Salespeople have never had formal sales training
- Company is at least ten years old
- Decision maker is VP of Sales/CEO
- Technology company
- Telecommunications company
- Printers/web designers/graphics company
- Realtors (100 percent commissions)
- Mortgage Brokers (100 percent commission)
- Financial Planners (100 percent commission)
- Insurance Agents (100 percent commission)
- Network marketers (100% commission)
- One person entrepreneurs

What do you think?

I look forward to speaking with you soon.

Sincerely,
Todd B. Natenberg

Author of, *"I've been in sales for 10 years! Now what?"* A (NEW Playbook for Skyrocketing Your Commissions)

Endorsed by Brian Tracy, Roger Dawson and Stephan Schiffman

President, TBN Sales Solutions

Phone: (816) 876-9184
e-mail: todd@toddnatenberg.com
http://www.toddnatenberg.com
www.ijustgotajobinsales.com

TBN Sales Solutions increases commissions for salespeople through customized training. We establish step-by-step sales processes with private workshops, individual consulting and keynote speaking for associations to impact the bottom line.

"Customers do not care how much you know until they know how much you care. But showing how much you care includes showing how much you care about yourself. Sell how you want to buy."

There are several important things to note about this letter:

- *Subject Line*

Networking is a different animal, so even though they may know your name in theory, remind them exactly how you met, where you met and the circumstances. Again, it's great organization, and will have them open up the e-mail.

- *Body of e-mail*

Make it short and sweet. You are sending an attachment because it shows professionalism. Don't waste words here with your benefit statement or website. They almost certainly will read it on the phone.

- *Ideal client*

Why not? While you are not asking for their business you are asking if they approach the same people you do. Include it in the e-mail. Remember they will read the e-mail if they are interested. Besides, it has happened more than node where what starts as a networking discussion does turn into a client/seller relationship. Go for it!

- *Signature*

Make it complete, as always. If they are interested, your contact information is right there at the bottom. They will know how to find you, where to click and what phone number to call- if they care. Even if you are sending this from your phone which we often do, include a complete signature. Here's a good strategy:

- Create a signature in the "notes" section under "productivity" in your Smartphone
- Copy and paste it accordingly when you send e-mails

NETWORKING/NO INTEREST FOLLOWUP E-MAIL

Subject: Chamber of Commerce friend/TBN Sales Solutions President says great meeting you in person

So-and-So,

It was great meeting you recently at the chamber of commerce event. I enjoyed our discussion very much. I hope you received as much out of the event as I did.

While I know we are in different worlds, should you hear of any companies or organizations looking for top-notch sales trainers, please keep me in mind. I'd greatly appreciate the help.

To reiterate, my ideal client is:

- Fifty to five hundred employees
- 10 to 100 salespeople
- $5 million–$100 million in annual revenues
- Outside salespeople who call on accounts in person
- Multiple locations with headquarters in a major city
- Salespeople have never had formal sales training
- Company is at least ten years old
- Decision maker is VP of Sales/CEO
- Technology company
- Telecommunications company
- Printers/web designers/graphics company
- Realtors (100 percent commissions)
- Mortgage Brokers (100 percent commission)
- Financial Planners (100 percent commission)
- Insurance Agents (100 percent commission)
- Network marketers (100% commission)
- One person entrepreneurs

I look forward to speaking with you soon.

Sincerely,
Todd B. Natenberg

Author of, *"I've been in sales for 10 years! Now what?"* A (NEW Playbook for Skyrocketing Your Commissions)

Endorsed by Brian Tracy, Roger Dawson and Stephan Schiffman

President, TBN Sales Solutions

Phone: (816) 876-9184
e-mail: todd@toddnatenberg.com
http://www.toddnatenberg.com
www.ijustgotajobinsales.com

TBN Sales Solutions increases commissions for salespeople through customized training. We establish step-by-step sales processes with private workshops, individual consulting and keynote speaking for associations to impact the bottom line.

"Customers do not care how much you know until they know how much you care. But showing how much you care includes showing how much you care about yourself. Sell how you want to buy."

6. Send PAL before the formal appointment

As we discussed earlier, send a PAL even for a networking meeting. (See Build the Business Case chapter for details). You think a prospect is impressed with a PAL? Check out how your networking partners react. It's huge!

7. Conduct the appointment in a non-lunch atmosphere

Contrary to conventional practices, never ever network over lunch! When you meet over lunch, both parties focus on eating. Neither can fully pay attention to the subjects at hand.

> *If you network over lunch, you will fill your stomach, but not your pocketbook. What is multitasking? Ignoring what's really important.*

On the other hand, don't have a networking meeting in an office if you can avoid it. Whoever has the office is now on higher ground. You want to be equal. After all, you are only trying to help one another. Coffee shops or Panera Bread type restaurants where you probably won't drink coffee or eat are best.

Running a networking meeting is identical to running a sales call. In essence, a networking appointment is a continuation of the initial meeting you had at the event prior. Only now you have each other's undivided attention, without others distracting you.

Another difference is that you talk in terms of your fellow networker's associates or clients, instead of how your services will help the person with who you are speaking. Remember that you are not trying to close the person in front of you. But you are trying to get the wheels rolling in terms of how that person can refer you, and how you can refer them.

One of the biggest mistakes people make on a networking call is forgetting that they still are there to conduct business. Networking is just a different kind of business.

So what do you ask when you have a networking meeting versus a sales meeting?

- "What has been the key to your success?"
- "What is your biggest challenge?"
- "Who is the ideal client for you?"

We discussed defining the ideal client earlier in the chapter. It's good to ask it again on the coffee visit even though you asked it when you first met. It's still effective because it emphasizes your interest in networking.

- "So how can I help you?"

Asking how you can help the person is done for a different reason. Often, while on a networking call, the person sitting across from you could be a prospect. But again they do not expect to be treated that way, nor should you. This question measures whether that person is interested in your services without asking outright.

For instance, the answer to "how can I help you?" could be one of two: (1) "If you come across clients looking for…" or (2) "I'm not really sure, but I do think my company may need your services…" TBN Sales Solutions has earned more than one client that way.

8. Follow up with a 3-way referral (as stated in referral chapter)

You do this one time and one time only. If they don't respond, move on quickly. You add them to your e-mail list and connected on LinkedIn. But that's it. They will be a time suck. You just gave them a gift and they can't even say thank you or acknowledge? Then, move on. The flip side, though, is if they respond and it garners business, now they are your best friend. Make the first move!

Whoever makes the first move in networking, the first offer to help, and provides the other one a referral to increase their revenues gets credit for the win/

> *win/win situation: you, them and the person to who you are referring them.*

Here's some additional Do's and don'ts of networking

- *Always have business cards with you.*

No excuses. Keep business cards in your briefcase, your car, your gym bag, your wallet and in your desk at work. Always have at least ten. Have a minimum of thirty when attending a formal networking event. You never know when or where opportunities will surface. Napkins with e-mails and phone numbers get lost easily.

- *Have e-mail on your business card and make sure another person can write on one side of the card you give*

If you design your own business cards, take advantage of important strategies. This may sound trite, but there are still people without e-mail addresses listed on their business cards. In this day and age, there is no excuse for not having an e-mail address on your card. E-mail is an integral tool if you are in sales. How can you network with someone who does not know how to reach you? Don't tell me that they can go to your website and look it up. Make it easy for them.

Along the lines of e-mail, you should never have a Gmail, Google, Yahoo or AOL account as your primary e-mail. It shouts amateur and unprofessional. How much would you invest in someone with a Yahoo account if they can't even afford their own business website?

Lastly, make sure another person can write on your business card. Fancy cards that are special paper may sound cool, but they aren't nearly as effective as you think. Practical is more powerful than cool.

- *Give a card/get a card.*

Some people say that handing out two cards is ideal because the recipient will keep one and give one to a prospect for you. The idea is solid, but the practice creates clutter- especially in this day and age of electronics. Your only goal is for them to take your card, record the information and then throw it out anyway. Now you are going to ask them to do it twice?

Also, assuming someone wants to refer your business without knowing much about you or what you can do can, giving two cards can be a big turnoff. Once you conduct the initial appointment on neutral turf, hand out a stack of cards to your new ally- if requested.

- *Always have pen and paper in addition to your Smartphone*

You'd be amazed how many people don't have something with which to write. Ideally, you'll take notes on the business card you just received. If you need more space, have paper handy. No one expects you to remember everything, but the more information you can reference, the stronger your position. Smartphones are great, but still have old school tools.

- *Always have your date book (probably a no brainer in Smartphone day and age, but worth repeating)*

If you can avoid phone tag and e-mail tag, do. Always be prepared to schedule an appointment. Let the other person look unprofessional.

So what did we learn about networking:

1. **Understand what it takes to network**

2. **Decide with whom to network**

3. **Know what to say when networking**

4. Schedule formal "coffee" appointment (if beneficial)

5. Follow up via e-mail

6. Send PAL before the formal appointment

7. Conduct appointment

8. Follow up with a 3-way referral

> *"Success has nothing to do with what you gain or accomplish for yourself. It's what you do for others."* – **Danny Thomas**

CHAPTER 10:

Professional Development

> Professional Development: Continuous exploration of new ideas to grow our qualities and reduce our faults both professionally and personally.

When we stop growing, we stop dreaming. When we stop dreaming, we stop living life to the fullest.

Why is it that the most successful people in the world always credit their success to others? Great presidents have great advisers, great athletes have great coaches, and great business people have great mentors. Do you notice a pattern?

To truly be successful, ongoing improvement is a must. It's no surprise that often salespeople's biggest slumps come after their biggest successes. They think they know it all, rest on their laurels, and forget to constantly improve. Don't stop learning.

Years ago, *Time* magazine wrote a cover story about how Tiger Woods reinvented his swing shortly after winning the Masters tournament. He worked on his swing with his coach while he was ranked the top golfer in the world!

For the next year or so, you did not hear much about Tiger. He won his share of tournaments and was still ranked number one. But the year after, Tiger's career reached unimaginable heights. He won what is now known as the Tiger Slam: four major golf tournaments held consecutively over a one-year period.

In this final chapter, we will present the playbook for ongoing development:

1. **Improve your own buying habits**
2. **Watch other selling habits**
3. **Read – but selectively**
4. **Classroom sales training**
5. **Take risks**

1. Improve your own buying habits

Throughout this book, we have repeatedly emphasized "sell how you want to buy." If you are an impulsive buyer, you will be an impulsive seller. If you are a meticulous buyer, you may be a meticulous seller.

Impulsive sellers usually do not fear asking for the order. They have a sense of urgency, which will transmit itself to the buyer.

But meticulous sellers are often reluctant to ask for orders, or even to advance the sales process. They empathize that if they were the buyer, they probably would not buy the product on the first appointment. Meticulous sellers sometimes delay the sales process unnecessarily. Often they tell their managers, "I can't be pushy like that. I can't do that to the customer." What they fail to understand is they wouldn't be "doing" anything, but helping.

> *Selling is helping. Give yourself credit. You are serving another person. Is there anything more honorable?*

While styles vary, to succeed in sales, certain personality traits must be stressed, such as persistence, confidence, and perseverance. Though the execution of the sale may vary, the required characteristics are the same for each transaction.

So the question is: how do we improve our buying habits—if we should at all?

> *A sale is not a science, but an art. Science is knowledge that Albert Einstein was born with. A sale is an art that can be perfected.*

Improvement begins with awareness. If you are a meticulous buyer, it doesn't mean you have to suddenly start buying impulsively. It just means that you must recognize this as a limitation in your selling habits.

One of the best ways to recognize this is to pay close attention when you purchase items. Notice what you like about the salesperson when you buy. Notice the result of your own practices. Why do you buy? What do you buy? You'll be amazed at the similarities between selling clothes in a store and selling a $10,000 product.

To illustrate this point, let's conduct an exercise involving negotiating at a retail store. The results will astound you.

PROFESSIONAL DEVELOPMENT

EXERCISE #PD1—NEGOTIATING RETAIL

- Prepare

Be prepared to make a little scene. People may stare. You won't be rude, but you may draw attention. Expect it. If you aren't willing to take this risk, stop now. But I do CHALLENGE you that if you take the chance to conduct this exercise, the results will be amazing.

The person who never makes a mistake probably isn't doing anything. Maybe you didn't succeed, but failure can be just as good. Isn't that how top salespeople measure themselves?

- Introduce yourself to a salesperson.

Find a salesperson to help you. Ask that person's name and, with a firm handshake, introduce yourself. State the person's name once again, adding, "Nice to meet you, So-and-So. I was wondering if you could help me."

You probably are the first person in the last six months—or ever—to actually ask their name, let alone treat them with respect. They will be flattered more than you can imagine.

- Request the manager by asking for "help."

Don't waste your time talking to someone who can't reduce the price. Retail salespeople often are guaranteed to say "no" because they can't say "yes." They usually have no vested interest in whether you purchase the item. Their hourly wage is unaffected by your purchase.

But someone in that store does care. With the salesperson's help, you need to get to that person.

As you've already been respectful, this shouldn't be an issue. But you do have to stand firm. You also don't want to further explain why you are asking for the manager, because if you say you want a price reduction, they will assume the role of decision maker, even though they aren't.

Here's how it works:

You: "So-and-So, I'd like to speak to the manager, please. I have a question about this item."

Salesperson: "What is it? Perhaps I can answer it."

You: "I appreciate that, but I'd like to speak to the manager. Thanks for your *help*."

- Introduce yourself to the manager, asking for help once again

The manager is expecting an angry customer, because why else would someone ask for the manager? Your salesperson may have explained you are not a lunatic, as you were very courteous to the salesperson, but still, managers are usually called to address problems. Watch the manager's surprise when you are calm, pleasant, and actually compliment the salesperson who helped you.

You: "Are you the manager?"

Manager: "Yes."

You: "What's your name? My name's Todd. [Shake hands.] It's nice to meet you, So-and-So. I was speaking with salesperson So-and-So, who was very helpful. But I had a question for you. I was wondering if you could *help* me too."

Manager: "Well, that depends. What can I do for you?"

You now have the manager's undivided attention. Managers might suspect you will ask them to reduce the price, but you have approached it professionally and politely.

PROFESSIONAL DEVELOPMENT

Also, you may be the first one to ever have done it this way. At this point, the manager is wishing more buyers would act like you.

What have you done thus far? You have actually not asked for a thing, but you have complimented the employee, the manager, and the store overall.

- Explain why you feel you deserve the price reduced

Now you need to create a reason why the manager should lower the price. But don't ask for a price reduction outright. Leave it open a little to speculation. The speculation will arise from your questions. Your argument may not be strong, but do make an argument. Here are some suggestions for wording:

- **"I have a question. Does this ever go on sale? Oh, it does? Since I'm here now, is there any chance you could help me? I don't want to be watching the ads for the next few months. I'd really appreciate the help."**

- **"It's more than I wanted to spend. I shop here all the time. Can you *help* me?"**

- **"I've seen it for less elsewhere. It's really the one I want. But I shop here all the time. Can you *help* me?"**

Notice the "Can you help me?" question repeatedly. You haven't actually asked for a price reduction, although you've implied it. All you are asking for is help- and we certainly have established that everyone wants to help.

If the manager seems confused about what you're asking, continue by saying, "Can you help me out on the price?"

At this point, one of a few things will happen. The manager will say yes, no, or silence, which is the most common.

If it is silence, what did we learn to say? Nothing! Just like objection handling, the manager is now thinking about your request. If you interrupt, you are dead in the water.

- Challenge

If you don't succeed, don't be confrontational. Challenge the manager's answers, but only to a degree. If you get the discount, it won't be because of your argument. It will be because the manager likes you based on the other steps you took.

If you say you've seen it for less elsewhere, the manager might suggest that you bring in the ad so the store can honor the competition's price. Don't let it get to that point. You will lose all credibility. Here's a recommendation:

"I appreciate that, So-and-So, but I admit I don't have the ad. I don't even know if it was the same item or when it was on sale. It was similar. That's all I know. I don't really want to race home to get it. Can you help me out?"

- Thank the manager- whether the price is reduced or not

If you succeed in getting the discount, whatever the discount is, take it. You are miles ahead of everyone else. Be happy. If you don't succeed, that's still okay. Thank the manager anyway. Take the item, proceed to the register and still buy the item, assuming you meant to in the first place regardless of a reduction. Your goal was not really to save money, although that's a nice benefit when this works! You were really practicing being the buyer.

The other reason to thank the manager no matter what the outcome is that you have not yet walked out the door. You never know what might happen by the time you get to the register.

Not only have I been successful with this exercise more than 50 percent of the time, but there have been some occasions when the manager followed me to the payment counter and then gave me a discount. The manager was so shocked by my sincerity, he couldn't resist helping me—after I had already agreed to buy the item at full price.

- Additional thank-you to the manager upon exit

Even if you do not get a discount, find the manager again and salesperson and thank them. You will feel better. So will they.

2. Watch other selling habits

Sell how you want to buy.

The next time you purchase items, observe the sellers. Ask yourself questions. What do you like about them? What don't you like? Do you like if they talk fast? Do you like if they talk slow? Why do salespeople never ask your name? How does it make you feel when they do? When they ask if they can help you, how does that sound?

Recently, I was at a restaurant when the cashier said, "Can I help the next guest?" We know the power of the word "help." How did "guest" make me feel? Pretty good.

Here's another example, again in real estate. Rob was my realtor some time ago and a close personal friend. I was one of Rob's first sales when he sold me my condominium in Chicago.

Two months after moving in, he asked me for a letter of recommendation. "I have a favor to ask of you. I need your help," he said. I wrote the letter on the spot.

The following suggests people in occupations you know. Think about them in terms of their selling skills. What do you like about them? What don't you like about them? What characteristics can you isolate that influence how you feel about them? What characteristics do they have that relate to their selling skills?

Who can serve as role models to learn good- and bad-selling skills?

Accountants
Bus drivers
CEO of your company/other companies
Customer service representatives
Doctor
Dry cleaner
Family
Fictitious television characters
Fireman
Friends
Fundraisers
Grocery clerk
Hair stylists
Help desk (your own/another)
Journalists conducting television interviews
Judges
Landlord
Lawyers
Police officer
Politicians
Priest/Rabbis/Minister
Retail store clerk/salesperson
Restaurant Manager/Server
Sales director/manager/salesperson at your own company
School teachers
School principals
Social worker
Talk show hosts
Taxi driver

3. Read- but selectively

Those who read are those who lead.

Someone once said that a book is a combination of a writer's persona and expertise, wrapped into a portable package you can carry with you. You can access that author whenever you want just by opening the book. Television may be entertaining and informative, but don't neglect books, newspapers, newsletters, and periodicals.

Commit to being a lifelong learner. Read at least one book every two months. Pick whatever titles interest you, but include some business books in your selection.

Read your local city newspaper, business magazines, and selling magazines. Pick those that are most interesting for you.

There are also some terrific free publications on the Internet. Virtually all newspapers enable you to receive free headlines on a daily basis. Wherever you live, subscribe via e-mail to your local newspaper. Pick and choose the ones you find most appropriate. You can't beat the price and the ease. Take advantage of your computer.

But let me caution you as well. In the 10 years since our first book has come out, we know the world has changed. Do NOT read everything. Eliminate the noise. Make sure what you are reading makes you a better person, a better salesperson, and enables you to contribute to the betterment of humanity.

When deciding which books to read or which internet articles to subscribe, monitor your emotions after you read articles, topics and themes. Ask yourself the following:

- What did I learn?
- How will this help me in life?
- How will this help me in my current/future job?
- How did reading this theme/topic/article make me feel?
- Did it make me frustrated or more productive?

While reading with your eyes is terrific, also take advantage of audio books. In today's world, it's quite easy and not that expensive to turn your car into an audio library. Download audible.com to your Smartphone and listen to books while driving to and from appointments.

4. Utilize classroom sales training

While often the best training comes in the field, don't discount the value of the classroom. Strategic theory is very useful. Theory enables you to bounce ideas off colleagues, experts, and others you respect. Isn't that why you are reading this book?

The type of sales training you select is up to you. But be sure you actively train at least one day a month. Keep your skills fresh in a group environment. If your manager won't pay for training, pay for it yourself. It's worth it in the long run. One full day a month, at least, is recommended.

Webinars/conference calls in today's fast paced technology are better than nothing, if that's what your schedule or finances allow. But I CHALLENGE you once again to recognize that what made you successful in the first place was your desire to learn from others to implement those strategies to make them your own. That only came from live interaction.

5. Take risks

By nature, salespeople must take risks. Any time you cold-call a prospect, any time you ask for an order, any time you pick up the phone, you are risking someone refusing you. The fact is that 99 percent of a salesperson's job involves others refusing their ideas. But notice the words. It's not rejection. It's not failure. It's a refusal of their ideas—or actually their services. Encompass your selling philosophy in your everyday life.

Take risks. Try new things. Make a pact with yourself, here and now, that once a month you will try something new. You pick the specific activity, but let it be something you wouldn't have tried before you read this book.

PROFESSIONAL DEVELOPMENT

Life's lessons come from daily events. But our greatest lessons come from things that we do not experience every day.

Conclusion

So what'd you think? Did you remember all this? Some you heard before. I'm sure a lot was new. So, what's next? The key now is to implement what you just learned.

I CHALLENGE you once again! You are among the elite: The Salesperson. You are once again the best of the best. When you achieve in sales, you achieve in all aspects of your life. Sales directly reflect the world in which we live.

Life is filled with ups and down. The key is to cherish those peaks and survive those valleys. Selling is no different.

But we must never forget what it takes for us to succeed.

When we recognize our formula for success, it's critical that we repeat and repeat again. It's a never-ending circle, one in which we love and will continue to love. Our process, our playbook, our grand plan, when executed, enables us to achieve all we want, all we desire, and all we deserve.

So, John, sure it has been 10 years and you may have seen lost. But it's time to get back to who you are, who you were and who you will be once again.

Remember this final thought:

> *Whenever I get down and depressed and think all of my work is for not, I think of a stonecutter. He spends his entire life chipping at stones and never sees a dent. Then one day, he taps the stone and the entire*

object breaks. But what he must never forget is were it not for the first million whacks, the stone never would have broken.

About the Author

As the president and founder of TBN Sales Solutions (TBNSS), Todd Natenberg increases commissions for salespeople through customized training. He establishes step-by-step processes with private workshops, individual consulting, and keynote speaking for associations to impact the bottom line.

A former sales manager, sales trainer, and award-winning salesperson in telecommunications, education, and consulting, Todd has done it all. He has sold everything from voice and data services, online K-12 and higher educational curriculum, photocopiers, wheelchair accessible minivans and shoes. Todd has worked the $20 transactional item to the $600,000 government account.

His career includes top performances at ATT, Qwest Communications, the Discovery Channel's education division, and Canon Business Solutions.

A graduate of the University of Missouri-Columbia School of Journalism, Todd began his career as a newspaper reporter. He served a Pulliam Fellowship at *The Arizona Republic* in Phoenix, was a staff writer for the *Daily Herald* in suburban Chicago, and covered telecommunications as a staff writer for the *Kansas City Business Journal*.

Over the years, Todd has been featured in *Sales and Marketing Executive Report*, written a regular column for *Selling!* magazine, and been featured on various radio and television stations, including *ABC7 News* and Tony Parinello's *Selling Across America*.

In 2007, Todd completed the Ironman Triathlon, a `141 mile race, in Wisconsin. In an astounding 16 and ½ hours, he swam 2.4 miles in open water, biked 112 miles and ran a 26.2 mile marathon.

"I've been in sales for 10 years! Now what?" A (NEW) Playbook for Skyrocketing Your Commissions is Todd's third book. In addition to his previous book, *"I just got a job in sales! Now what?"* Todd is the author of *The Journey Within: Two Months on Kibbutz*, which chronicled his adventures of self-discovery volunteering on an Israeli kibbutz in 2000. He also has published the e-book, *"Why won't they call me back?"*

Todd recently produced the home study 10 hour interactive cd course *How to Double Your Sales in ½ the Time: Sell how you want to buy*.

In addition to sales training, Todd is a motivational speaker who talks to groups and organizations about self-discovery, fatherhood and personal growth.

He lives with his wife Reena, a University piano professor, and their amazing twin sons Ari and Teddy in suburban Kansas City. Todd also writes a fatherhood column for various publications sharing his amazing experiences loving Ari and Teddy.

Visit www.toddnatenberg.com and www.ijustgotajobinsales.com to learn more about TBN Sales Solutions. You also can contact Todd at (816) 876-9184 or e-mail todd@toddnatenberg.com.

Want TBN Sales Solutions Live?

TBN Sales Solutions increases commissions for salespeople through customized training. We establish step by step processes through private workshops, individual consulting and keynote speaking for associations to impact the bottom line.

TBN programs range from five days to half a day and include the following topics:

How to Double Your Productivity in ½ the Time (Goal Setting/Time Management)
How to Double Your Prospects in ½ the Time (Prospecting)
How to Triple Your Sales Without Hiring a Soul (Referrals)
How to Double Your Sales in ½ the Time (Running a sales appointment)
How to Skyrocket Others' Sales; How they will Skyrocket Yours (Networking)
How to Seize a Buying Opportunity (Objection Handling)
The Lure of Leadership (Leadership)
Walk the Walk (ride along on in person meetings/conference calls)
"I just got a job in sales! Now what?" (keynote/workshop)
Bad Economy? Sell Your Way Out Of It! (keynote/workshop)
Why won't they call me back? (keynote/workshop)
No More Cancellations! (keynote/workshop)

In addition, TBN develops customized sales tools and provides consultative services in the following areas:

- Written personalized sales playbooks
- Assessment, analysis, recommendations (verbal and written)
- Ride along
- Individual sales consulting

TBN brings a unique approach to the sales training process. Combining humor with personal and professional success stories, President Todd Natenberg pulls from all facets of life to teach the art of selling. A self-described "facilitator," Todd has designed programs that are extremely interactive and entertaining. From Hollywood movies to newspaper articles to traditional role plays, nothing is out of bounds for Todd. Past students describe him as "charismatic, energetic, and a true professional."

For more information on TBN Sales Solutions, please call (816) 876-9184 or e-mail todd@toddnatenberg.com. Visit www.ijustgotajobinsales.com for more information.

Additional Praise for TBN Sales Solutions...

"I always thought of myself as a good salesperson, but I wanted to become a great salesperson. I use a lot of the skills you showed me as second nature. The same skills have also helped me in my personal life, which is an added bonus. I truly believe in your training course and encourage all my loan officers to attend. Thanks for all your great help and effort."

Chuck Sowers, President, American Mortgage Werks, Inc.

"I've signed new consulting contracts and brought on new clients using techniques and ideas that you have taught. My overall approach to sales is much more structured and effective after having your sales coaching. I'll be honest. Initially, I was skeptical, but I can say now it well worth the time and money. I would highly recommend you to anyone wishing to get a better grasp of the sales process or to refine their marketing and sales strategy."

Nathan Laurell, Partner, Technacity, LLC

"Your seminar was great. I was able to articulate my business message in a clear and concise manner for the first time. I learned new techniques. It also was a great review. Being a former sales manager, I know the importance of all three. Your seminar has enabled me to speed up the development of my new business. You are a tremendous facilitator, and I would recommend you to anyone."

Paul Baraz, Director of Fun and Games, Actualization Enterprises, Strategic Organizational Interventions

"Since your first visit, we have noticed heightened awareness of personal and professional goals, more employee conversation about teamwork, and more interaction between employees and management. Thanks again for the insight and inspiration, which your leadership and team building training has provided our company. It has become a valuable asset to the way we do business at Wadsworth Pumps."

James Wadsworth, Director of Operations, Wadsworth Pumps, WJ. Wadsworth and Associates, Inc.

"I would like to extend my heartfelt thanks for the outstanding presentation you presented to our management staff members. I can't tell you how energized our people were as a result of your program. I look forward to working with you in the future. Your passion, energy, and commitment to helping people grow is inspiring."

Leslie Smigel, Property Manager, Century Point Luxury Apartment Homes

"Since participating in your seminars less than a month ago, we have had a record month in sales. The simple but powerful tools we learned have helped us gain a new momentum and will give us the confidence to maintain it. Thank you for putting together a great seminar series."

Alex Puig, CEO, Allied Computer Training Center

"The feedback I have received from our staff after your Time Management seminar was very positive. I don't write recommendation letters unless I see tangible results from my staff at least one to two months after any presentation. However, I just had a staff meeting, and sure enough, a large percentage of the staff is still using the time management techniques you presented at our corporate off-site. I appreciated your presentation techniques, and I know the majority of the staff found your presentations entertaining and informative."

Mark J. Cleaver, CEO, Technomic International

ADDITIONAL PRAISE FOR TBN SOLUTIONS...

"I liked having the opportunity to gather together as a group and discuss different tactics and methods. I liked best the role playing and then having everyone's evaluations. You were good. You helped everyone get involved."

Stephanie Urbanski, Account Executive, CyberSearch Ltd.

Also by Todd Natenberg

The Journey Within: Two Months on Kibbutz

In the summer of 2000, Todd B. Natenberg, a thirty-year-old resident of Chicago, quit his job as a sales manager and sales trainer, started his own sales training company, sold his house, and finalized a divorce. But before embarking on his new career and life, he took the adventure he had always wanted: volunteering on an Israeli kibbutz.

By venturing to the most contentious of places and submersing himself in one of the world's oldest and richest cultures—his heritage—Todd teaches us about how true fulfillment comes from our connections with others.

The Journey Within: Two Months on Kibbutz is for anyone who has questioned the meaning of life.

"*A personal journal of an intrepid individual with a big heart and open mind who dove in headfirst to learn a lot about himself and others. The Journey Within: Two Months on Kibbutz is not so much a story about Israel. It's about relationships with others and the impact they have on us.*"

Aaron Cohen, Editor, *JUF News*

"*Where is a heart to feel from one's heart? In* The Journey Within, *Todd Natenberg fearlessly recounts a journey that few of us are willing to undertake. It's exhilarating to go along for the ride.*"

John Kador, author of *Charles Schwab: How One Company Beat Wall Street and Reinvented the Brokerage Industry*

"Todd is someone who loves and enjoys people. His thoughts on the kibbutz are fascinating. His insights into all those he met are very revealing. It's amazing how those he met could trigger such depths of emotions. We should all learn Todd's lessons."

Michael Wynne, Past President of National Speakers Association—Illinois

"A terrific book. The Journey Within: Two Months on Kibbutz *is not only Todd's story and his search for answers. It's also a wonderful insight into life on a kibbutz and the diverse people who live and work on it.*"

Rita Emmett, Author of *The Procrastinator's Handbook: Mastering the Art of Doing It Now*

"In his journey to a kibbutz and his journey since, Natenberg has discovered that nothing feeds the soul like a small world made larger."

Brad Herzog, Author of *States of Mind* and *Small World*

Copies of *The Journey Within: Two Months on Kibbutz* can be purchased online where all fine books are sold or by calling (877) 823-9235.

www.ingramcontent.com/pod-product-compliance
Lightning Source LLC
Chambersburg PA
CBHW031435160426
43195CB00010BB/741